The Art of Self-Transformation:
Strategies for Personal Growth and Fulfillment

To my beloved parents, your resilience and support shaped me. Despite faults, I forgive and appreciate you. This book is a testament to your love and inspiration. Thank you for being my greatest teachers. I can honestly say, I now understand… And I apologize for any and every inconvenience I've ever caused you.

"In recognizing the humanity of our fellow beings, we pay ourselves the highest tribute."

-Shirley Chisholm

Foreword

In "The Art of Self-Transformation: Strategies for Personal Growth," Jaynene Mercer, an army veteran and activist, offers a profound exploration into the journey of self-discovery and personal development. With wisdom born from her own experiences and insights, Mercer guides readers on a transformative odyssey, inviting them to embark on a path of self-awareness, resilience, and empowerment.

Throughout these pages, Mercer shares practical strategies and profound reflections, encouraging readers to embrace vulnerability as a catalyst for growth, cultivate self-compassion amidst adversity, and live with intentionality and authenticity. Drawing from her background as an army veteran and activist, Mercer infuses her narrative with lessons learned from overcoming challenges and confronting societal injustices, offering readers a road map for navigating life's complexities with grace and resilience.

"The Art of Self-Transformation" is not merely a book; it is a beacon of hope and empowerment for all those seeking to unlock their true potential and live with purpose. As readers embark on this transformative journey, may they find inspiration, guidance, and courage within these pages, knowing that the power to transform their lives lies within their own hands.

-LTMilton Robert Walters III, USN,

Acknowledgement

I am profoundly grateful to my beloved husband, Rob, for his unwavering support, love, and encouragement throughout this journey. Your strength and belief in me have been a constant source of inspiration.

To my three incredible children, RJ, Khloe, and King, you bring boundless joy and laughter into my life every day. Your presence fills my heart with warmth and purpose, and I am endlessly proud to be your parent.

I extend heartfelt appreciation to my mother-in-law, Cathy Mercer, whose strength and resilience have taught me invaluable lessons in navigating life's challenges with grace and determination. Your tough love and unwavering support have shaped me in profound ways, and I am grateful to have had your presence in my life. You are greatly missed.

To my siblings, each of you holds a special place in my heart. To my oldest brother, Milton Robert Walters III, thank you for being my best friend, my source of guidance, and a pillar in my life and my best friend. To my younger brothers Byron, Brandon, and Kwame, may wisdom guide you on your journey, and may you soar to heights beyond imagination. To my sisters Zha-nee and Tamiyah, may you inherit the blessings God has aligned for you, and may your beautiful souls continue to shine brightly. And to my sisters Jayne and Shafone, may God's wisdom and blessings enrich your lives abundantly. I love you all dearly.

Table of Contents

Introduction	13
Understanding Self-Transformation	17
Cultivating Self-Awareness	25
Embracing Self-Acceptance	33
Nurturing Self-Improvement	40
Transformative Practices	48
Cultivating Positive Relationships	57
Overcoming Obstacles	64
Allowing Yourself to Forgive	77
Sustaining Growth and Fulfillment	84
Embracing Growth	95
About the Author	105
Also by Jaynene Mercer	106

Introduction

I felt myself slipping into the unknown, and that was my biggest fear at the time: the unknown. My anxiety had been skyrocketing, and I knew a breakdown was imminent if I didn't get a handle on it soon. So, I told myself, "Jaynene, whatever it is, pray about it and let it go." I knelt down, praying for God to show me a sign of what he wanted me to do next. After praying and shedding tears, still unsure why I felt so low when my life seemed fine, I felt a sense of relief wash over me. Picking up my phone, I scrolled through social media, but with each swipe, my heart seemed to pound harder against my chest. I couldn't understand why, so I set my phone aside and lay on my couch, tears filling my eyes, still grappling with the exact problem.

Out of the corner of my eye, I spotted my bookshelf, filled with books. Memories flooded back of my childhood habit of seeking solace in reading whenever I felt troubled or overwhelmed. So, I stood up, grabbed the first book I saw—whether I'd read it before didn't matter; I just needed to read. And I did. I read the entire weekend, only stopping for sleep and meals, never once touching my phone again.

After immersing myself in serious reading for an entire weekend, I finally I stumbled upon a book that sparked a revelation for me—one about personal growth and self-discovery. It was a lightbulb moment when I realized what I'd been missing: the concept of self-transformation. The stories within these books fueled my soul, especially those of individuals who had faced adversity and emerged stronger. That's when I knew I had to begin my own journey of self-exploration.

One book that resonated deeply with me was Charlamagne Tha God's "Shook One." His candid accounts of grappling with anxiety and

insecurity hit home for me. Reading about his journey to overcome those fears inspired me to confront my own demons head-on. Then there was "Atomic Habits" by James Clear. This book completely shifted my perspective on habits and their impact on our lives. Clear's practical advice on cultivating positive habits and breaking negative ones equipped me with the tools to make meaningful changes in my daily routine. On the last day, of the weekend, I read "Ready for Revolution" by Stokely Carmichael (Kwame Ture) left a profound impact on me. His impassioned call to action for social change stirred something deep within me, reminding me that transformation isn't just about personal growth; it's also about effecting change in the world around us.

It took me a day to read each book, and after each reading session, I'd take time to meditate in my office, allowing my thoughts to flow freely. It was during these moments of reflection that I found clarity and direction, guiding me toward the next steps on my journey of self-discovery and growth.

One pivotal moment stands out in my memory: the day I decided to confront my fear of failure and pursue a long-held dream of starting my own business. Despite the doubts and uncertainties that plagued my mind, I took a leap of faith and launched my venture. The journey was far from easy, filled with setbacks and challenges, but through perseverance and self-reflection, I gradually began to transform both my business and myself. As I reflect on that transformative period of my life, I realize the profound impact that self-transformation has had on my sense of purpose and fulfillment. By embracing change and stepping outside of my comfort zone, I discovered strengths and abilities I never knew I possessed. And while the journey of self-transformation is ongoing, I am grateful for the lessons learned and the person I continue to become.

It is from this place of personal experience and growth that I invite you to explore the art of self-transformation with me. Together, let us embark on a journey of discovery, healing, and empowerment as we unlock the limitless potential within ourselves. In the journey of life, there exists a profound opportunity for individuals to evolve, grow, and become the best versions of themselves. At the heart of this transformative process lies the concept of self-transformation – a deliberate and conscious effort to undergo inner change for the sake of personal growth and fulfillment.

Self-transformation is more than just a journey; it's an art form that requires dedication, courage, and self-awareness. It involves examining our beliefs, behaviors, and perceptions with a critical eye, and then actively working to reshape them in alignment with our true selves. Why is self-transformation so crucial? Because it holds the key to unlocking our full potential and living a life of meaning and purpose. By embracing change and continuously striving to better ourselves, we open doors to new opportunities, deeper connections, and greater fulfillment. In a world where external pressures and expectations often dictate our actions, self-transformation empowers us to reclaim ownership of our lives. It allows us to break free from self-imposed limitations, heal past wounds, and chart a course towards a future filled with possibility.

Throughout this book, we will explore the various strategies, tools, and practices that can aid in the process of self-transformation. From cultivating self-awareness to nurturing positive relationships, each chapter will offer insights and guidance to support you on your journey towards personal growth and fulfillment.

So, are you ready to embark on this transformative adventure? Prepare to discover the art of self-transformation and unlock the potential that lies within you.

Practical Exercise:

1. *Take a few moments to reflect on your current relationship with yourself. Consider how you typically talk to yourself and treat yourself on a daily basis.*

Reflection Prompt:

1. *What are your initial thoughts and feelings about embarking on a journey of self-transformation and personal growth?*

Understanding Self-Transformation

Defining Self-Transformation and Its Components

  I must be honest; there's no moving forward without acknowledging my past behavior. I used to harbor what can only be described as the worst attitude imaginable. Reflecting on those moments now, I realize that in many cases, my attitude was completely unwarranted. I allowed my emotions to dictate my reactions, often without considering the consequences or the impact my behavior had on others. It's humbling to admit, but I recognize the hurt and frustration I may have caused with my negativity and hostility. Taking full accountability for my past actions is a necessary step in my journey of self-transformation. It's only by confronting these uncomfortable truths that I can truly begin to change and grow as a person. Self-awareness is a pivotal aspect of self-transformation, enabling individuals to observe, understand, and reflect upon their thoughts, emotions, and behaviors. For me, the journey of self-awareness began with a profound realization rooted in my childhood experiences and where my attitude stemed from. Growing up as a child of abuse—both physical and emotional—I found myself navigating a tumultuous environment shaped by my father's strict discipline and my mother's emotional instability.

  My father, a traditional West Indian man, believed in authoritarian parenting, instilling fear through physical punishment and strict adherence to his rules. I vividly recall the terror of sitting on a metal chair, frozen in place as the blows from his disciplinary measures rained down upon my brothers and me. Meanwhile, my mother, though loving in her own way, struggled with emotional instability and a penchant for prioritizing her romantic relationships over her children.

The realization that I had been using my childhood trauma as a crutch to dictate how I lived in the present hit me like a ton of bricks. It stirred up a complex mix of emotions—sadness for the pain endured, frustration for allowing it to shape my actions, and a profound sense of relief in acknowledging the truth. I had been carrying the weight of my past on my shoulders, allowing it to influence my decisions and perceptions of myself and others. Recognizing this pattern was a transformative moment in my journey of self-awareness. It allowed me to step back and examine the underlying fears and beliefs that were driving my behavior. I realized that, despite the dysfunction of my upbringing, I had the power to break free from the cycle of trauma and forge a new path for myself.

Armed with this newfound insight, I embarked on a journey of introspection and healing. I began to challenge the narratives ingrained in me from childhood and redefine my sense of self-worth and identity. Through therapy, self-reflection, and inner work, I gradually let go of the notion that my past experiences defined my present reality.

This newfound self-awareness empowered me to make conscious choices aligned with my values and aspirations. It allowed me to cultivate healthier relationships, set boundaries, and pursue personal growth with intentionality. While the scars of my past will always be a part of me, I no longer allow them to dictate my present or future. Instead, I embrace my journey of self-transformation with courage and resilience, knowing that each step forward brings me closer to a life of authenticity and fulfillment.

Self-transformation is a multifaceted process that lies at the heart of personal growth and development. It involves a deliberate and conscious effort to evolve, adapt, and improve oneself on various levels. At its core, self-transformation encompasses the journey of self-discovery, inner exploration, and the cultivation of a deeper understanding of oneself. This process is not static but rather dynamic, unfolding over time as individuals navigate the complexities of their inner and outer worlds.

One crucial component of self-transformation is self-awareness. Self-awareness involves the ability to observe, understand, and reflect upon one's thoughts, feelings, and behaviors. It entails being attuned to one's inner experiences, motivations, and values, as well as recognizing how these factors influence one's actions and interactions with others. Through self-awareness, individuals gain insights into their strengths, weaknesses, and areas for growth, empowering them to make more informed choices and live with greater intentionality.

Self-acceptance is another fundamental aspect of self-transformation. It entails embracing oneself fully, with all of one's perceived flaws, imperfections, and vulnerabilities. Self-acceptance involves letting go of self-criticism, judgment, and unrealistic expectations, and instead, cultivating a sense of compassion, kindness, and unconditional positive regard towards oneself. It is about recognizing and honoring one's inherent worth and inherent dignity, regardless of external circumstances or societal standards. Through self-acceptance, individuals can experience greater peace, contentment, and authenticity in their lives.

Do you recall at the beginning of this book when I shared the moment I was scrolling through Instagram and felt my heart pounding in my chest? It was a stark realization of how deeply I had immersed myself in social media, constantly comparing my life to the curated highlight reels of others. In that moment, I was blind to the beauty of my own journey, fixating instead on an illusion of success and fulfillment.

I came to realize that I had been measuring my accomplishments against someone else's 30-second highlight reel, failing to appreciate the richness of my own story. Here I am, in my thirties, happily married to the father of my children, who adore me unconditionally. As an army veteran and a successful business owner, I've defied the odds as a Black woman, owning two thriving beauty supply stores in Georgia and soon to open another in Pennsylvania. Beyond my professional achievements, I am deeply invested in giving back to my community. I visit prisons to advocate for financial literacy and mental health, leveraging my degrees in psychology and business management to empower others. My journey has been shaped by resilience and a steadfast commitment to fighting for the rights and equality of my people.

Yet, despite these accomplishments, I found myself trapped in a cycle of self-doubt and criticism. I would mentally berate myself, unable to see my own worth beyond the lens of comparison. There were moments when I couldn't bear to look at myself, picking apart every flaw and imperfection. It took time, introspection, and a deep reckoning with my inner critic to realize that I was enough just as I am. I had to learn to appreciate and embrace Jaynene in all her complexity and beauty. I had already surpassed the limitations that society had imposed on me, so why was I allowing myself to be defined by someone else's standards of success?

Through this journey of self-acceptance and self-love, I discovered the power of recognizing my own worth and celebrating the unique path I've walked. It's an ongoing journey, but each day brings me closer to a place of true appreciation and authenticity.

Self-improvement is a key driving force behind self-transformation. It involves the active pursuit of personal growth, development, and enhancement in various areas of life. Self-improvement encompasses setting goals, acquiring new skills, and making positive changes to enhance one's well-being, fulfillment, and overall quality of life. It is about continuously striving to become the best version of oneself, both personally and professionally. Self-improvement efforts may focus on areas such as physical health, mental well-being, relationships, career advancement, and spiritual growth. Through self-improvement, individuals can unlock their full potential, overcome obstacles, and achieve their aspirations.

Self-transformation is a dynamic and holistic process that involves self-awareness, self-acceptance, and self-improvement. These components work synergistically to facilitate personal growth, fulfillment, and overall well-being. By cultivating self-awareness, embracing self-acceptance, and actively engaging in self-improvement efforts, individuals can embark on a journey of profound inner transformation, leading to greater authenticity, resilience, and empowerment in their lives.

Cultivating self-awareness in daily life involves practicing mindfulness and reflection. It begins with paying attention to our thoughts, emotions, and actions without judgment. Mindfulness practices such as meditation, journaling, or simply taking moments of pause throughout the day can help cultivate a deeper understanding of ourselves. By observing our thoughts and behaviors, we can identify patterns, triggers, and underlying beliefs that shape our experiences. Through consistent practice, we can develop a heightened sense of self-awareness that empowers us to make more intentional choices and navigate life with greater clarity and insight.

Practicing self-acceptance, especially during challenging times, requires patience, self-compassion, and vulnerability. It involves embracing all aspects of ourselves, including our flaws, mistakes, and vulnerabilities, with kindness and understanding. Rather than denying or resisting difficult emotions or experiences, self-acceptance encourages us to acknowledge them with compassion and non-judgment. This process may involve reframing negative self-talk, practicing self-care, and seeking support from others. By cultivating self-acceptance, we can foster a greater sense of inner peace, resilience, and authenticity in our lives.

Determining which areas of our lives could benefit from self-improvement requires reflection, goal-setting, and prioritization. It involves assessing our strengths, weaknesses, values, and aspirations to identify areas where we seek growth or change. Setting SMART (Specific, Measurable, Achievable, Relevant, Time-bound) goals can help clarify our intentions and create a roadmap for progress. Prioritizing areas that align with our values and long-term objectives allows us to focus our energy and resources effectively. By taking consistent action towards our goals, we can gradually improve various aspects of our lives and create meaningful change.

There are several practical techniques and exercises that can enhance self-awareness, self-acceptance, and self-improvement. These may include mindfulness meditation, self-reflection journaling, gratitude practices, visualization exercises, and setting intentions. Mindfulness meditation involves focusing on the present moment and observing our thoughts and sensations without attachment. Self-reflection journaling allows us to explore our thoughts, feelings, and experiences in writing, gaining insights and clarity. Gratitude practices involve cultivating appreciation for the positive aspects of our lives, fostering a mindset of abundance and contentment. Visualization exercises involve mentally rehearsing desired outcomes and envisioning our future selves, motivating and guiding us towards our goals. Setting intentions involves clarifying our values and priorities, guiding our actions and decisions with purpose and alignment.

Cultural and societal influences can significantly impact one's ability to engage in self-transformation. Cultural norms, beliefs, and values shape our perceptions of self and others, influencing how we view success, happiness, and personal growth. Societal expectations, stereotypes, and pressures may create barriers to self-expression, authenticity, and acceptance. Additionally, systemic inequalities and social injustices can affect access to resources, opportunities, and support for personal development. Recognizing and challenging cultural and societal norms that limit our potential or constrain our choices is essential for fostering inclusive and equitable spaces for self-transformation.

While self-transformation can be pursued independently, professional guidance or support can offer valuable insights, accountability, and resources. Therapists, coaches, mentors, or spiritual advisors can provide guidance, perspective, and personalized strategies for navigating challenges and achieving goals. Professional support can help individuals gain clarity, overcome obstacles, and develop effective coping skills and tools for self-awareness, self-acceptance, and self-improvement. Additionally, group settings such as support groups, workshops, or community programs offer opportunities for connection, shared learning, and mutual support on the journey of self-transformation.

Navigating resistance or fear during the process of self-transformation is a common challenge that requires courage, perseverance, and self-compassion. Resistance may arise from fear of change, uncertainty, or discomfort associated with confronting limiting beliefs or stepping outside of our comfort zone. Acknowledging and validating these feelings without judgment is the first step towards overcoming them. Practicing self-compassion involves treating ourselves with kindness and understanding, especially during times of struggle or setbacks. Cultivating resilience through mindfulness, positive self-talk, and self-care can help us navigate challenges and stay committed to our growth journey.

There are potential pitfalls or challenges to be aware of when embarking on a journey of self-transformation. These may include perfectionism, self-doubt, burnout, and the tendency to compare ourselves to others. Perfectionism can create unrealistic expectations and hinder progress by focusing on flaws rather than achievements. Self-doubt may undermine confidence and motivation, leading to procrastination or avoidance of challenges. Burnout can occur when individuals push themselves too hard without adequate rest or self-care, leading to exhaustion and decreased effectiveness. Comparing ourselves to others can erode self-esteem and detract from our unique strengths and contributions. Awareness of these challenges allows us to cultivate resilience, self-compassion, and healthy coping strategies to navigate them effectively.

The duration of the self-transformation process varies widely depending on individual circumstances, goals, and commitment levels. While some changes may occur relatively quickly, others may require sustained effort and patience over an extended period. Staying motivated and committed throughout the journey of self-transformation involves setting realistic expectations, celebrating small wins, and cultivating self-compassion. Reflecting on progress, adjusting goals as needed, and seeking support from others can help maintain momentum and overcome obstacles. Embracing the process as a continuous journey of growth and learning allows individuals to stay engaged and resilient amidst challenges and setbacks.

Self-reflection plays a crucial role in the process of self-transformation, providing opportunities for insight, learning, and growth. Incorporating self-reflection into daily routines allows individuals to pause, observe, and evaluate their thoughts, emotions, and actions. Journaling, meditation, or contemplative practices can facilitate self-reflection by creating space for introspection and inner dialogue. Asking open-ended questions such as "What am I feeling? What do I need? What can I learn from this experience?" encourages deeper self-awareness and understanding. By regularly engaging in self-reflection, individuals can gain clarity.

Embarking on a journey of self-transformation can be a profoundly rewarding experience, offering numerous benefits that extend across various aspects of life. One of the key advantages is the cultivation of self-awareness. Through introspection and reflection, individuals gain a deeper understanding of their thoughts, emotions, and behaviors. This heightened self-awareness provides clarity and insight into personal strengths, weaknesses, and patterns, enabling individuals to make more informed choices and navigate challenges with greater resilience.

Another significant benefit of self-transformation is the promotion of self-acceptance. By embracing oneself fully, including both strengths and imperfections, individuals develop a sense of compassion and self-love. This acceptance fosters inner peace and reduces self-criticism, allowing individuals to cultivate a more positive and nurturing relationship with themselves. As a result, they experience greater contentment and authenticity in their interactions with others and the world around them.

Self-transformation also facilitates personal growth and development. Through intentional efforts to improve and evolve, individuals expand their skills, knowledge, and capabilities. They set meaningful goals, overcome obstacles, and stretch beyond their comfort zones, leading to increased confidence and fulfillment. Moreover, self-transformation empowers individuals to align their actions with their values and purpose, fostering a greater sense of meaning and fulfillment in life.

Additionally, embarking on a journey of self-transformation can have ripple effects that extend beyond the individual. As individuals grow and evolve, they often inspire and uplift those around them, contributing to positive changes within their communities and beyond. By embodying authenticity, resilience, and compassion, they become catalysts for transformation and positive change in the world.

The benefits of embarking on a journey of self-transformation are vast and far-reaching. From cultivating self-awareness and self-acceptance to fostering personal growth and inspiring others, the rewards are both intrinsic and extrinsic. By embracing the journey of self-transformation, individuals unlock their full potential, lead more meaningful lives, and contribute to a brighter and more compassionate world.

Practical Exercise:

1. *Create a vision board or collage that represents your ideal self and the changes you'd like to make in your life.*

Reflection Prompt:

1. *How do you envision your life transforming as you embark on this journey of self-transformation?*

Cultivating Self-Awareness

In the whirlwind of running my business while juggling shifts at Northside Hospital, stress and anxiety became my constant companions. Each day felt like a relentless battle against the clock, leaving me mentally drained and yearning for a moment of respite. Amidst the chaos, finding a sense of peace seemed like an impossible feat. That's when I started mindfulness meditation. Admittedly skeptical at first, I decided to give it a shot, hoping for some relief from the overwhelming pressure. Sitting quietly, I attempted to quiet the racing thoughts and swirling emotions, allowing myself to simply be in the present moment. Initially, it felt awkward, almost unnatural, as if my mind was resisting the stillness. But with time and persistence, something incredible happened.

I began to notice subtle shifts in how I approached challenges. Instead of getting swept away by stress, I found myself observing it from a distance, like watching clouds pass in the sky. Slowly but surely, I learned to navigate the ups and downs of daily life with a newfound sense of clarity and calmness. Beyond the professional realm, mindfulness meditation touched every aspect of my life. It transformed the way I interacted with others, allowing me to listen more deeply and empathize more authentically. My relationships flourished as I became more present and attuned to the needs of those around me.

But perhaps the most profound impact was the sense of inner peace it brought me. In the midst of life's chaos, mindfulness became my sanctuary—a place where I could retreat and find solace, even if just for a few precious moments. It taught me that true well-being isn't found in external circumstances, but in the ability to cultivate peace within ourselves, no matter what storms may rage around us.

Mindfulness meditation is a practice that involves bringing focused attention to the present moment. By sitting quietly and observing our thoughts, emotions, and bodily sensations without judgment, we can cultivate greater self-awareness. Mindfulness meditation allows us to become more attuned to the fluctuations of our mind and body, helping us recognize patterns and triggers that influence our behavior and reactions. Through regular practice, we develop the capacity to respond to life's challenges with greater clarity and equanimity. Mindfulness meditation offers a path to self-discovery and personal transformation, enabling us to live more fully and authentically.

Journaling is a powerful tool for self-reflection and introspection. By writing down our thoughts, feelings, and experiences, we create a space for self-expression and exploration. Journaling allows us to externalize our inner world, gaining clarity and insight in the process. Whether through free writing, structured prompts, or gratitude journaling, journaling provides a means to track our growth, identify recurring themes, and uncover hidden beliefs or assumptions. By making journaling a regular practice, we deepen our understanding of ourselves and our lived experience, fostering greater self-awareness and resilience.

Asking ourselves probing questions is a technique for deepening self-awareness. By posing open-ended questions, we invite introspection and self-inquiry. Questions such as "What am I feeling right now? What are my core values? What patterns do I notice in my behavior?" encourage us to explore our thoughts, emotions, and motivations more deeply. Self-reflection questions serve as a catalyst for self-discovery and personal growth, helping us gain clarity and insight into our inner world. By engaging with self-reflection questions regularly, we develop a habit of introspection that enriches our lives and relationships.

I remember years ago I was at a crossroads, facing one of those life-altering decisions that keep you up at night. The pressure was intense, and I felt like I was drowning in a sea of uncertainty. It was a pivotal moment, and I knew I needed some clarity, pronto. So, I decided to do some soul-searching, armed with nothing but a barrage of questions aimed straight at the heart of the matter. What did I really want? What were my deepest desires? What were the values I refused to compromise on?

As I dug deeper into my own psyche, it was like turning on a light in a dark room. Suddenly, things started to make sense. I began to see myself more clearly, to understand what truly mattered to me. With each question, I felt a little more empowered, a little more sure of myself. It wasn't just about making a decision anymore—it was about honoring who I was, deep down inside. And when I finally made my choice, it felt like coming home. It was a decision made from a place of authenticity, of self-awareness. And let me tell you, it was the best decision I ever made. So, if you ever find yourself facing a tough decision, don't be afraid to ask yourself those tough questions. You might just find the answers you've been searching for all along.

Body scan meditation is a mindfulness practice that involves systematically bringing awareness to different parts of the body. By scanning through the body from head to toe, we can observe sensations, tensions, and areas of relaxation. Body scan meditation fosters greater awareness of the mind-body connection, helping us recognize how our physical state influences our emotional well-being. Regular practice of body scan meditation enhances our ability to tune into bodily cues and cultivate a deeper sense of embodiment. As we become more attuned to our bodies, we can respond to stress and discomfort with greater ease and compassion, fostering overall well-being and resilience.

Utilizing reflective writing prompts encourages self-awareness and insight. Reflective writing prompts prompt us to explore specific themes or experiences in depth. Examples of reflective writing prompts include "Describe a time when you felt most alive. What values do you hold most dear? What are your greatest fears and how do they manifest in your life?" Reflective writing prompts stimulate introspection, enabling us to gain clarity on our values, beliefs, and aspirations. By engaging with reflective writing prompts, we deepen our understanding of ourselves and our lived experience. Through the practice of reflective writing, we cultivate a habit of self-inquiry that enriches our lives and fosters personal growth.

Exploring beliefs, values, and motivations is a crucial aspect of cultivating self-awareness. Here are some strategies for delving into these core aspects of oneself:

1. Reflective Journaling: Journaling allows individuals to explore their beliefs, values, and motivations in a private and introspective manner. Set aside time regularly to write about experiences, thoughts, and emotions related to significant events or decisions in your life. Reflect on how these experiences have shaped your beliefs and values, and examine the underlying motivations driving your actions.

2. Questioning Assumptions: Take time to question your assumptions about yourself and the world around you. Ask yourself why you hold certain beliefs or values, and whether they align with your authentic self. Challenge any beliefs that no longer serve you or that may be based on outdated information or societal expectations.

3. Values Clarification Exercises: Engage in values clarification exercises to identify and prioritize your core values. Consider what principles are most important to you and why. Explore how these values influence your decision-making process and guide your behavior in various areas of your life, such as relationships, career, and personal development.

4. Mindful Reflection: Practice mindful reflection by bringing focused attention to your beliefs, values, and motivations in daily life. Set aside moments of quiet contemplation to observe your thoughts, feelings, and intentions without judgment. Notice any patterns or themes that emerge and reflect on how they contribute to your sense of identity and purpose.

5. Seeking Feedback: Seek feedback from trusted friends, family members, or mentors to gain insight into how others perceive your beliefs, values, and motivations. Listen with an open mind to their perspectives and consider how their feedback aligns with your self-perception. Use this feedback as an opportunity for self-reflection and growth.

6. Exploring Personal Narrative: Reflect on your personal narrative—the story you tell yourself about who you are and how you fit into the world. Consider how your beliefs, values, and motivations have evolved over time and shaped your life experiences. Explore how rewriting your narrative can lead to greater self-awareness and empowerment.

By actively exploring beliefs, values, and motivations, individuals can deepen their self-awareness and gain valuable insights into their innermost selves. This process of exploration lays the foundation for personal growth, authenticity, and alignment with one's true purpose in life.

Let me take you back to a pivotal moment in my life—the decision to get married. It was a decision fraught with fear and uncertainty, shaped by the tumultuous relationships I had witnessed growing up. With my parents, siblings, and even extended family members experiencing multiple failed marriages, I couldn't help but feel apprehensive about taking the plunge myself.

But amid the fear, there was also a deep-rooted determination—a determination to break the cycle of broken relationships and create a loving, stable home for my children. I knew that if I wanted to build a strong foundation for my family, I had to first understand and love myself. So, I embarked on a journey of self-discovery—a journey that involved exploring my likes, dislikes, strengths, and weaknesses. I learned to value and appreciate myself, recognizing that true love begins with self-love. And as I embraced my authenticity, I found myself attracting someone who saw and loved me for who I truly was.

Meeting my husband felt like destiny—a series of serendipitous events that aligned perfectly with God's plan for us. From living just around the corner from each other to sharing the same family values and life goals, every sign pointed towards our union being ordained by a higher power. And when my husband confidently declared his intention to marry me from the moment we met, I knew that he was either crazy or our love was destined to be. Our wedding day marked not just the beginning of our journey together but also a profound realization of life's purpose and the true meaning of love. It was through loving and accepting myself that I was able to recognize and embrace the next phase of my life with clarity and conviction. And in the arms of my husband, I found a love that reaffirmed my belief in the power of authenticity, faith, and destiny.

Looking back on my journey, I've come to realize just how vital it was to explore my beliefs, values, and motivations. It wasn't always easy, but by delving into the depths of who I am, I unearthed hidden patterns and beliefs that shaped my decisions. Questioning these beliefs allowed me to align my choices with my true self, giving me a clearer sense of purpose. Similarly, reflecting on my values helped me prioritize what truly matters in life, guiding me through tough decisions. Understanding my motivations provided insight into my deepest desires and aspirations, helping me distinguish between passion-driven actions and those influenced by external factors. This journey of self-discovery has been transformative, filled with moments of growth and enlightenment. Today, I stand rooted in my values, guided by my beliefs, and fueled by a sense of purpose that propels me forward. Though it took courage and dedication to embark on this path of self-awareness, the personal growth and fulfillment I've gained along the way have made it all worthwhile.

Embarking on a journey of self-awareness can be both empowering and challenging. For some individuals, the prospect of introspection may evoke discomfort or fear of facing difficult emotions or truths about themselves. In this chapter, we will explore the importance of self-compassion and non-judgmental awareness in overcoming resistance to introspection and embracing self-awareness practices with an open mind and gentle curiosity. Resistance to introspection often stems from a fear of confronting aspects of ourselves that we may perceive as undesirable or painful. It can be tempting to avoid delving into our inner world to avoid discomfort or maintain a sense of self-protection. However, it is precisely through this process of self-exploration that we can uncover valuable insights and foster personal growth.

Self-compassion is the foundation of self-awareness practices. It involves treating ourselves with kindness, understanding, and acceptance, especially in moments of difficulty or vulnerability. By cultivating self-compassion, we create a supportive inner environment that allows us to approach introspection with gentleness and kindness, rather than harsh self-judgment.

Non-judgmental awareness is another essential aspect of self-awareness practices. It involves observing our thoughts, emotions, and experiences without attaching judgment or evaluation. Instead of labeling our thoughts or feelings as good or bad, right or wrong, we simply acknowledge them with curiosity and openness, allowing them to arise and pass away naturally. When engaging in self-awareness practices, it's important to approach them with an open mind and gentle curiosity. Instead of viewing introspection as a task to be completed or a problem to be solved, see it as an opportunity for self-discovery and growth. Embrace the process with a sense of wonder and exploration, allowing yourself to learn and evolve along the way.

There are many ways to cultivate self-compassion in daily life. Engage in activities that bring you comfort and joy, such as spending time in nature, practicing mindfulness, or engaging in creative expression. Practice self-care rituals that nourish your body, mind, and spirit, such as getting enough sleep, eating nutritious food, and engaging in physical activity. It's natural to encounter difficult emotions during introspection, but remember that these emotions are not a reflection of your worth or value as a person. Instead of suppressing or denying them, allow yourself to fully experience them with compassion and acceptance. Reach out for support from trusted friends, family members, or mental health professionals if needed.

Remember that self-awareness is a journey, not a destination. Celebrate your progress and growth along the way, even if it's small. Embrace the imperfections and setbacks as opportunities for learning and development. By approaching self-awareness practices with self-compassion and non-judgmental awareness, you can cultivate a deeper understanding and acceptance of yourself, leading to greater peace, fulfillment, and authenticity.

Practical Exercise:

1. *Practice mindfulness meditation for 10-15 minutes daily, focusing on observing your thoughts, emotions, and bodily sensations without judgment.*

Reflection Prompt:

1. *What insights have you gained about yourself through practicing mindfulness and self-awareness?*

Embracing Self-Acceptance

In the journey of self-awareness, one of the most profound and transformative practices is that of self-acceptance. It involves embracing ourselves fully, with all our strengths, weaknesses, and imperfections. Self-acceptance is the ability to acknowledge and embrace all aspects of ourselves, including our thoughts, feelings, and experiences, without judgment or criticism. It involves recognizing our inherent worth and value as human beings, regardless of our flaws or past mistakes. Self-acceptance does not mean complacency or resignation; rather, it is about acknowledging reality as it is and choosing to respond with kindness and compassion towards ourselves.

Transitioning from the concept of self-awareness, let's delve into the transformative journey of self-acceptance. Many individuals struggle with inner criticism, constantly berating themselves for perceived shortcomings or failures. This critical inner voice can undermine self-confidence and perpetuate feelings of unworthiness. Challenging our inner critic is a journey toward self-compassion and self-acceptance. By recognizing the voice of our inner critic, we can begin to challenge its validity and cultivate a more nurturing inner dialogue. It's essential to remind ourselves that making mistakes is an inherent aspect of the human experience. Instead of berating ourselves for our flaws, we can choose to embrace them as opportunities for growth and learning.

As we navigate the landscape of self-awareness, inner criticism often emerges as a formidable obstacle. Practicing self-kindness involves treating ourselves with the same warmth and understanding that we would offer to a close friend. When faced with self-criticism, we can counteract it with gentle reminders of our inherent worth and value. By acknowledging our mistakes without judgment, we create space for self-compassion to flourish. Remembering that self-acceptance does not require perfection can be liberating. It allows us to release the unrealistic expectations we may place on ourselves and embrace our humanity in all its complexity.

Counteracting this inner critic requires a shift towards self-compassion and acceptance. Cultivating self-compassion involves extending understanding and forgiveness to ourselves, especially in moments of vulnerability. Rather than dwelling on our shortcomings, we can choose to focus on our efforts and intentions. This shift in perspective can help us break free from the cycle of self-criticism and foster a greater sense of self-acceptance. Embracing our imperfections with kindness and empathy allows us to embrace our authentic selves more fully. As we navigate life's challenges with self-compassion, we cultivate a deeper sense of resilience and inner strength.

Practicing self-kindness is a vital aspect of nurturing self-acceptance within ourselves. Acknowledging our struggles is the first step toward self-compassion and healing. It's essential to recognize that everyone faces challenges and setbacks at various points in their lives. Instead of dismissing or minimizing our difficulties, we can honor our experiences and emotions with honesty and compassion. By acknowledging our struggles, we validate our feelings and create space for healing and growth. Remember that it's okay to feel overwhelmed or uncertain at times; these emotions are a natural part of the human experience.

Offering ourselves words of encouragement and comfort is a powerful practice that can help soothe our inner turmoil. When we're facing difficulties or self-doubt, it's easy to fall into a pattern of self-criticism and negativity. However, by consciously choosing to speak to ourselves with kindness and compassion, we can shift our inner dialogue toward one of self-acceptance and support. Remind yourself that you are worthy of love and kindness, regardless of your perceived flaws or shortcomings. You deserve to treat yourself with the same warmth and understanding that you would offer to a dear friend in need.

Acknowledging our struggles becomes a cornerstone in the journey towards self-compassion and healing. During times of difficulty or self-doubt, it's crucial to practice self-compassion and self-care. This means prioritizing your well-being and taking steps to nurture yourself emotionally, mentally, and physically. Engage in activities that bring you joy and comfort, whether it's spending time in nature, practicing mindfulness meditation, or enjoying a favorite hobby. Remember that self-care is not selfish; it's an essential aspect of maintaining your overall health and happiness.

In moments of adversity, offering ourselves words of encouragement becomes a powerful practice. It's also helpful to cultivate a sense of gratitude for the strengths and resilience that have carried you through challenging times in the past. Reflect on moments when you've overcome obstacles or demonstrated courage in the face of adversity. Recognize the inherent strength within you and trust in your ability to navigate whatever challenges lie ahead. By acknowledging your past triumphs and acknowledging your struggles with kindness and compassion, you empower yourself to face the present moment with greater resilience and self-assurance.

Additionally, surrounding yourself with a supportive network of friends, family, or mental health professionals can provide valuable encouragement and guidance during difficult times. Don't hesitate to reach out for help when you need it; seeking support is a sign of strength, not weakness. Remember that you are not alone in your struggles, and there are people who care about you and want to see you thrive. By allowing yourself to receive support and encouragement from others, you open yourself up to the possibility of healing and growth.

Acknowledging your struggles and offering yourself words of encouragement and comfort are essential practices for cultivating self-compassion and resilience. Remember that you deserve love and kindness, especially during times of difficulty or self-doubt. By embracing your experiences with honesty and compassion, you create space for healing and growth to occur. Trust in your inner strength and resilience, and know that you are capable of overcoming whatever challenges life may bring.

Comparison is a common barrier to self-acceptance, as individuals often measure their worth against others' achievements or appearances. Letting go of the habit of comparison is a transformative practice that allows us to cultivate greater self-acceptance and inner peace. When we constantly compare ourselves to others, we diminish our sense of self-worth and create unnecessary suffering. It's important to recognize that each person's journey is unique, with its own set of challenges, triumphs, and lessons. By letting go of comparison, we can embrace our individuality and honor the path that we are meant to walk.

Comparing ourselves to others often leads to feelings of inadequacy or insecurity, as we focus on what we perceive to be our shortcomings or failures. However, it's essential to remember that our worth is not determined by external measures of success or achievement. We are inherently worthy simply because we exist, regardless of how we measure up to others. By shifting our focus inward and cultivating self-compassion, we can recognize and appreciate our own strengths and talents. It's natural to admire the accomplishments or qualities of others, but comparing ourselves to them can be detrimental to our well-being. Instead of viewing others as competition or benchmarks for our own success, we can choose to celebrate their achievements and find inspiration in their journeys. When we approach comparison from a place of admiration rather than judgment, we create a sense of camaraderie and connection with those around us.

One of the most powerful ways to let go of comparison is to practice gratitude for the unique gifts and blessings in our own lives. Take time each day to reflect on the things that bring you joy, fulfillment, and meaning. Whether it's the love of family and friends, the beauty of nature, or personal accomplishments, cultivating gratitude helps shift our focus away from what we lack and toward what we have. Another helpful practice is to cultivate self-awareness and mindfulness in our daily lives. Pay attention to the thoughts and emotions that arise when you find yourself comparing yourself to others. Notice any patterns or triggers that contribute to feelings of inadequacy or insecurity. By bringing awareness to these patterns, we can begin to challenge and reframe them, replacing self-criticism with self-compassion and acceptance.

It's also important to set realistic expectations for ourselves and recognize that perfection is unattainable. Each of us is a work in progress, continually growing and evolving over time. Embrace the journey of self-discovery and personal growth, knowing that setbacks and challenges are a natural part of the process. By letting go of the need to constantly measure up to others, we free ourselves to embrace our own unique path and experience greater fulfillment and happiness.

If you truly think about it, letting go of comparison is a practice of self-love and acceptance. It requires us to release the need for external validation and trust in our own worthiness. Remember that you are enough exactly as you are, and that your worthiness is not contingent on how you stack up against others. Embrace your uniqueness, celebrate your strengths, and trust in the beauty of your own journey. Gratitude can be a powerful antidote to self-doubt and criticism. Encourage readers to cultivate a daily gratitude practice, focusing on the things they appreciate about themselves and their lives. Remind them that acknowledging their strengths and accomplishments can help cultivate a greater sense of self-acceptance and fulfillment.

Fostering gratitude for our strengths can amplify our journey towards self-acceptance. Cultivating a daily gratitude practice focused on appreciating ourselves and our lives can truly transform our outlook and well-being. Each morning, take a moment to reflect on something you genuinely appreciate about yourself. It could be a personal quality, a recent accomplishment, or simply your resilience in facing life's challenges. By starting the day with self-appreciation, you set a positive tone and reaffirm your worthiness.

Remember, it's important to acknowledge both your strengths and your accomplishments, big or small. Often, we tend to downplay our achievements or focus on our perceived flaws. However, celebrating your successes and recognizing your unique qualities is essential for nurturing a positive self-image and boosting your self-esteem. Extend your gratitude practice beyond yourself to encompass various aspects of your life. Express gratitude for supportive relationships, meaningful experiences, or even the simple joys of everyday life. By acknowledging the abundance present in your life, you cultivate an abundance mindset and invite more positivity and fulfillment into your daily experience. Start incorporating moments of gratitude throughout your day, whether it's jotting down things you're thankful for in a journal or simply pausing to appreciate the beauty around you. By making gratitude a regular part of your life, you'll find yourself feeling more grounded, content, and at peace with yourself and the world around you.

Reaching out to others for support and encouragement has been instrumental in my journey towards self-acceptance. I've learned that I don't have to navigate life's challenges alone and that there are people who genuinely care about my well-being. Whether it's friends, family members, or a therapist, having a support system in place can provide comfort, guidance, and a sense of belonging during difficult times. It's essential to remind ourselves that seeking help is not a sign of weakness but rather a demonstration of strength and courage. Opening up about our struggles and vulnerabilities can be daunting, but it's the first step towards healing and growth. By reaching out to others, we give ourselves permission to be imperfect and acknowledge that we all need support from time to time.

Surrounding ourselves with supportive networks further nurtures our path towards self-acceptance. When seeking support, it's important to surround ourselves with people who uplift and encourage us. Choose individuals who offer empathy, understanding, and non-judgmental support. Whether it's a trusted friend who listens without judgment or a therapist who provides professional guidance, finding the right support network can make a world of difference in our journey towards self-acceptance. In addition to seeking support from others, it's also crucial to offer ourselves compassion and kindness. Often, we can be our harshest critics, but learning to treat ourselves with the same care and understanding we extend to others is essential for fostering self-acceptance. Remember that we are all human, and it's okay to make mistakes or face challenges along the way. By embracing support from others and practicing self-compassion, we create a nurturing environment where self-acceptance can thrive. Together, we can overcome obstacles, celebrate our progress, and cultivate a deep sense of acceptance and love for ourselves.

Reflecting on our journey, celebrating progress becomes an integral part of self-acceptance. As I reflect on my journey towards self-acceptance, I've come to realize the importance of celebrating every step of the way. It's essential to acknowledge and honor the progress I've made, no matter how small it may seem. Each achievement, no matter how minor, represents a triumph over self-doubt and fear. I encourage myself, and others daily, to take the time to recognize and celebrate our accomplishments. Whether it's overcoming a fear, challenging a negative belief, or simply showing ourselves kindness and compassion, every effort deserves acknowledgment. By celebrating our progress, we affirm our worthiness and reinforce our commitment to self-acceptance. It's important to remember that self-acceptance is an ongoing journey, not a destination. There will be setbacks and challenges along the way, but each step forward is a testament to our resilience and determination. By celebrating our progress, we affirm our ability to grow and evolve, even in the face of adversity.

Embracing our achievements reinforces our commitment to self-acceptance, highlighting its ongoing nature. As I celebrate my achievements, I also acknowledge the courage it takes to fully embrace myself. It requires vulnerability and bravery to confront our insecurities and fears, but the rewards are immeasurable. By celebrating my progress, I honor the strength and resilience that lies within me, and I reaffirm my commitment to living authentically and unapologetically. In the journey towards self-acceptance, every step forward is a victory worth celebrating. We have to take the time to acknowledge our progress, honor our growth, and embrace ourselves fully, just as we are.

Practical Exercise:

1. *Write a letter to yourself expressing unconditional acceptance and love, acknowledging all aspects of who you are.*

Reflection Prompt:

1. *How does practicing self-acceptance impact your self-esteem and overall well-being?*

Nurturing Self-Improvement

Nurturing self-improvement is a vital aspect of personal growth and fulfillment. This chapter explores practical strategies for setting realistic goals, embracing continuous learning and growth, and building resilience in the face of challenges. Determining realistic goals for personal development begins with a thorough self-assessment. Reflect on your strengths, weaknesses, interests, and values to pinpoint areas for growth. It's crucial to strike a balance between setting challenging goals and ensuring they're attainable within your current circumstances and resources.

Moving from self-assessment to goal setting, adopting the SMART criteria offers numerous advantages. Setting SMART goals for personal development provides clarity and focus. By clearly defining what you want to achieve and how you plan to do it, you establish a road map for success. Moreover, SMART goals are measurable, allowing you to track progress and maintain accountability. They're also relevant to your aspirations, ensuring your efforts are directed towards meaningful outcomes. Lastly, by incorporating deadlines, SMART goals foster a sense of urgency and motivation.

Illustrating SMART goals with examples showcases their versatility across various areas of personal development. Examples of SMART goals for personal development illustrate their adaptability to individual objectives. In career development, a SMART goal could be pursuing a certification in project management to enhance professional skills. In health and wellness, a SMART goal might involve losing a specific amount of weight within a defined time frame through lifestyle changes.

While setting ambitious goals is encouraged, finding a balance between challenge and achievability is paramount. Balancing achievability and challenge ensures that personal development goals stretch your abilities without becoming overwhelming. Strive for goals that push you out of your comfort zone while remaining within reach with effort and commitment. Avoid setting goals that are overly ambitious or unrealistic, as they may lead to frustration and demotivation if not achieved.

Implementing effective strategies is essential for staying on track toward achieving personal development goals. Staying on track toward personal development goals requires effective strategies. Break larger goals into smaller, manageable tasks, create a timeline or action plan, and regularly review progress. Seek support from mentors or accountability partners, and be open to adjusting strategies based on feedback and outcomes. When encountering obstacles, cultivating resilience and adaptability is key to overcoming challenges. When facing obstacles or setbacks, approach them with resilience and adaptability. View challenges as opportunities for learning and growth. Identify specific obstacles, brainstorm solutions, and adjust goals or strategies as necessary. Embrace setbacks as valuable lessons on the path to personal development.

Utilizing tools and resources facilitates progress tracking and maintains motivation in personal development. Numerous tools and resources are available to track progress and measure success in personal development. From journaling and goal-tracking apps to habit trackers and progress charts, choose methods that resonate with you. Aligning goals with values and priorities enhances their significance and relevance, fostering commitment and focus.

Accountability and celebration play pivotal roles in sustaining momentum and enthusiasm throughout the personal development journey. Accountability serves as a powerful motivator in achieving personal development goals. Whether through sharing goals with a trusted friend, joining a support group, or working with a coach, external accountability provides encouragement and guidance. Celebrating achievements, no matter how small, boosts morale, reinforces positive behaviors, and maintains momentum toward further goals.

Example: Sarah wants to improve her public speaking skills. She sets a SMART goal to enroll in a public speaking course, practice delivering speeches regularly, and participate in Toastmasters meetings to gain confidence and refine her skills.

Strategies for Continuous Learning and Growth:

Continuous learning is indeed fundamental for personal growth and development. Embracing a mindset of lifelong learning opens doors to new opportunities and experiences, fostering continuous growth. Individuals can explore a myriad of avenues to expand their knowledge and skills, ranging from traditional resources like books and workshops to modern platforms such as online courses and webinars. By actively seeking out learning opportunities, individuals can stay relevant in their fields and adapt to evolving trends and technologies.

Beyond traditional methods, experiential learning offers a dynamic approach to personal development. Experiential learning, characterized by hands-on experiences and real-world challenges, provides a dynamic approach to personal growth. By stepping out of their comfort zones and embracing new experiences, individuals can acquire valuable insights and skills. Whether it's traveling to unfamiliar destinations, taking on new hobbies, or volunteering for community projects, each experience offers opportunities for learning and growth. Embracing experiential learning allows individuals to develop resilience, adaptability, and a broader perspective on life.

Incorporating mentorship into one's learning journey provides valuable guidance and support. Mentorship is another powerful strategy for continuous learning and growth. By seeking guidance from experienced mentors or advisors, individuals can benefit from their wisdom, knowledge, and insights. Mentors can provide valuable feedback, share their experiences, and offer guidance on navigating challenges and opportunities. Through mentorship, individuals gain access to a wealth of expertise and resources, accelerating their learning and personal development journey. Additionally, mentoring relationships often foster mutual growth and development, as mentors learn from their mentees' unique perspectives and experiences.

Example: John is passionate about photography and wants to improve his skills. He subscribes to photography magazines, watches tutorials online, attends photography workshops, and practices taking photos regularly. By immersing himself in the learning process, he gradually enhances his photography skills and develops his unique style.

Building Resilience in the Face of Challenges:

Resilience is the ability to bounce back from setbacks and adversity. Building resilience involves developing coping strategies, maintaining a positive mindset, and seeking support when needed. Techniques such as mindfulness meditation, gratitude journaling, and cognitive reframing can help individuals navigate challenges more effectively.Resilience, often described as the ability to bounce back from setbacks and adversity, is a vital trait for navigating life's inevitable challenges. Building resilience involves developing coping strategies that enable individuals to withstand and overcome difficulties. One key aspect of resilience is maintaining a positive mindset, even in the face of adversity. By cultivating optimism and focusing on solutions rather than dwelling on problems, individuals can better navigate challenging situations and emerge stronger from them.

In addition to mindset, practicing techniques such as mindfulness meditation can enhance resilience. Mindfulness meditation is a powerful practice for building resilience and emotional well-being. By cultivating present-moment awareness and non-judgmental acceptance of one's thoughts and feelings, individuals can develop greater resilience to stress and adversity. Mindfulness meditation helps individuals build emotional regulation skills, allowing them to respond to challenges with clarity and composure. Through regular practice, individuals can develop a sense of inner calm and equanimity, enabling them to navigate life's ups and downs with greater ease and resilience.

Another effective technique for building resilience is gratitude journaling. Gratitude journaling involves regularly writing down things for which one is grateful. This simple practice can have profound effects on mental health and resilience. By focusing on the positive aspects of life, individuals can cultivate a sense of appreciation and resilience in the face of adversity. Gratitude journaling helps shift attention away from negative thoughts and emotions, promoting a more optimistic outlook on life. Research has shown that regularly practicing gratitude can improve overall well-being, enhance resilience, and reduce symptoms of depression and anxiety.

Cognitive reframing is another valuable tool for building resilience and overcoming adversity. Cognitive reframing involves challenging negative thought patterns and replacing them with more positive and empowering beliefs. By reframing negative situations in a more constructive light, individuals can develop a more resilient mindset and better cope with challenges. For example, instead of viewing a setback as a failure, individuals can see it as an opportunity for growth and learning. By changing their perspective, individuals can build resilience and develop a greater sense of self-efficacy, enabling them to bounce back from adversity more effectively.

Example: Emily experiences a setback at work when her project doesn't meet expectations. Instead of dwelling on failure, she practices resilience by reflecting on lessons learned, seeking feedback for improvement, and focusing on solutions rather than problems. Through resilience-building practices, she turns setbacks into opportunities for growth and development.

In my journey of personal growth and self-discovery, I've come to adopt a unique perspective on the concept of "goals." While the term is commonly used to signify milestones or achievements, I've found it limiting in capturing the essence of continuous improvement. Goals, by their nature, imply a sense of finality once achieved, leaving little room for further progression. However, I believe in the power of setting steps instead of rigid goals. Viewing personal development as a series of steps mirrors the ongoing nature of growth and transformation. Each step represents a forward movement, akin to ascending a ladder or climbing a flight of stairs. Like the never-ending staircase of the Empire State Building, there's always another step to take, another level to reach. This perspective allows for a more dynamic and fluid approach to self-improvement, where progress is not confined to the attainment of predefined goals but rather unfolds organically through continuous action and exploration. While I prefer the term "steps," I recognize that many individuals resonate with the term "goals." Therefore, I use both interchangeably, acknowledging that they represent the same journey of personal evolution. Each step taken is a deliberate choice towards growth and self-discovery.

When I first confronted my anxiety and early stages of depression, I turned to journaling as a means of self-exploration and transformation. Armed with a simple composition book, I began jotting down the steps I wanted to take each month to nurture my mental, physical, and emotional well-being. With each passing month, I noticed subtle yet profound shifts within myself. I discovered a nurturing side, a caring side, and a deeper level of self-awareness that had previously eluded me. Through the process of setting steps and taking deliberate actions towards my self-transformation, I unearthed layers of myself that I didn't even know existed. Each step became a catalyst for growth, propelling me forward on my journey of self-discovery. In embracing this approach, I found liberation from the confines of rigid goals and embraced the limitless potential inherent in the journey of continuous improvement.

Nurturing self-improvement is not merely a destination but a journey marked by commitment, effort, and a courageous embrace of change. By setting realistic goals, individuals lay the foundation for their personal growth endeavors, providing a clear roadmap toward their aspirations. Moreover, the pursuit of continuous learning and growth fuels this journey, offering endless opportunities for exploration, development, and expansion of one's capabilities. Additionally, building resilience serves as a formidable ally on this transformative path. In the face of challenges and setbacks, resilience acts as a shield, enabling individuals to weather storms and emerge stronger than before. Through the cultivation of resilience, individuals develop the inner strength and fortitude necessary to navigate life's inevitable obstacles with grace and perseverance. They learn to view setbacks not as roadblocks but as stepping stones, propelling them forward on their journey toward self-improvement.

In essence, nurturing self-improvement is about embracing a mindset of lifelong growth and fulfillment. It requires individuals to cultivate a willingness to step outside their comfort zones, confront their fears, and embrace the unknown. As they embark on this journey, they empower themselves to break free from limiting beliefs and societal expectations, unlocking their full potential in the process. Ultimately, by nurturing self-improvement, individuals not only enhance their own lives but also contribute positively to the world around them, inspiring others to embark on their own journeys of growth and self-discovery.

Transitioning from the broader concept of resilience-building techniques, I want to dive deeper into the specific cognitive-behavioral approach known as cognitive reframing. This technique offers individuals a structured framework for challenging negative thought patterns and cultivating resilience. By understanding how cognitive reframing works and its effectiveness in promoting resilience, you can gain valuable insights into overcoming adversity and enhancing emotional well-being.

Cognitive reframing is a powerful cognitive-behavioral technique that plays a pivotal role in building resilience and enhancing emotional well-being. At its core, cognitive reframing involves the process of challenging negative thought patterns and replacing them with more adaptive and empowering beliefs. By reshaping our perceptions and interpretations of challenging situations, cognitive reframing enables individuals to cultivate a more resilient mindset and navigate adversity with greater ease and confidence.

One of the key elements of cognitive reframing is the identification and correction of common cognitive distortions. These distortions, such as black-and-white thinking, catastrophizing, and personalization, often contribute to negative thinking patterns and undermine resilience. For example, black-and-white thinking involves viewing situations in extremes, such as seeing things as either entirely good or entirely bad, without recognizing shades of gray. Catastrophizing involves imagining the worst possible outcome of a situation, while personalization involves taking responsibility for events that are beyond one's control.

By reframing these cognitive distortions, individuals can gain a more balanced and realistic perspective on life's challenges. For instance, instead of catastrophizing about a minor setback at work, such as receiving constructive feedback on a project, individuals can reframe the situation by acknowledging it as an opportunity for growth and improvement. Similarly, rather than engaging in black-and-white thinking about their abilities, individuals can recognize their strengths and weaknesses as part of the human experience, leading to a more compassionate and resilient self-view.

Practicing cognitive reframing involves actively challenging negative thoughts and beliefs through cognitive-behavioral techniques. One common exercise is cognitive restructuring, which involves identifying irrational beliefs and replacing them with more rational and constructive alternatives. For example, if someone experiences anxiety about an upcoming presentation and thinks, "I'm going to fail miserably," they can reframe this thought by asking themselves, "What evidence do I have to support this belief?" and "What's a more realistic and helpful way to think about this situation?"

Research in cognitive-behavioral therapy (CBT) has consistently demonstrated the effectiveness of cognitive reframing techniques in promoting resilience and reducing symptoms of anxiety and depression. Studies have shown that individuals who engage in cognitive reframing exercises experience improvements in their ability to cope with stress, regulate emotions, and maintain a positive outlook on life. By incorporating cognitive reframing into their daily lives, individuals can develop greater resilience and well-being, enabling them to thrive in the face of adversity.

Practical Exercise:

1. *Set SMART (Specific, Measurable, Achievable, Relevant, Time-bound) goals for areas of personal growth and development.*

Reflection Prompt:

1. *What steps can you take to nurture your ongoing self-improvement journey and track your progress effectively?*

Transformative Practices

Embarking on my journey of personal growth and self-discovery has been incredibly rewarding, leading me to explore various enriching practices that have deeply impacted my sense of self-awareness, resilience, and fulfillment. In this chapter, I share insights into these empowering practices that have resonated with me and offer guidance on how they can enrich your own journey. These practices encompass a rich tapestry of disciplines, from ancient wisdom traditions to modern therapeutic modalities. Each practice goes beyond being a mere ritual; it's a pathway to personal evolution, offering profound insights and opportunities for growth. Whether it's mindfulness meditation, creative expression, or gratitude rituals, I've found that each holds the potential to catalyze profound shifts in consciousness, empowering me to navigate life's challenges with grace and authenticity.

Throughout history, cultures worldwide have embraced these transformative practices as vehicles for spiritual awakening and self-realization. From the ancient wisdom of Eastern philosophies to the contemplative practices of Western mystics, humanity has long recognized the empowering power of practices that cultivate inner peace, wisdom, and compassion. In today's fast-paced world, these practices have taken on renewed significance as I seek refuge from the stresses of modern life and strive to reconnect with my innermost self.

In this chapter, I invite you to join me on a journey of exploration and discovery as we uncover the transformative potential of mindfulness meditation, creative expression, gratitude rituals, and more. Drawing upon the latest research findings, expert insights, and real-life examples, we'll explore the profound impact of these practices on mental health, emotional well-being, and personal growth. Whether you're a seasoned practitioner or new to these enriching practices, there is much to discover and learn. Together, let's embark on this journey with open hearts and minds, embracing the empowering potential that lies within each of us.

Establishing daily habits is crucial for fostering self-transformation. These habits act as the building blocks of change, providing structure and consistency to our efforts towards personal growth. By integrating habits such as regular exercise, healthy eating, and adequate sleep into our daily routines, we create a strong foundation for positive transformation. These habits not only nourish our physical well-being but also support our mental and emotional resilience, empowering us to overcome obstacles and pursue our goals with confidence.

As we explore the importance of daily habits in supporting self-transformation, let's dive into the role of journaling prompts and exercises in facilitating self-discovery. Journaling serves as a powerful tool for self-reflection and exploration. Through prompts and exercises designed to evoke introspection, we can delve deeper into our thoughts, emotions, and experiences, gaining valuable insights into our inner world. By regularly engaging in journaling practices, we create a space for self-discovery and personal growth, uncovering hidden patterns, beliefs, and desires. Whether it's journaling about our dreams and aspirations, reflecting on past challenges and triumphs, or expressing gratitude for the present moment, these exercises guide us on a journey of self-awareness and transformation.

Building on the practice of journaling, let's explore the transformative potential of mindfulness, meditation, and visualization in our daily lives. Mindfulness, meditation, and visualization offer powerful techniques for cultivating presence, clarity, and intention in our daily lives. By incorporating these practices into our routines, we can cultivate a deeper sense of awareness and connection with ourselves and the world around us. Mindfulness encourages us to be fully present in each moment, fostering a sense of peace and acceptance. Meditation provides a space for quiet reflection and inner stillness, allowing us to tap into our innate wisdom and intuition. Visualization empowers us to create a mental blueprint for our desired outcomes, harnessing the power of imagination to manifest our dreams into reality. Together, these practices offer a holistic approach to personal growth and transformation, supporting us on our journey towards fulfillment and self-realization.

Numerous studies have demonstrated the beneficial effects of mindfulness meditation on mental health. Research indicates that regular mindfulness meditation practice is associated with reduced symptoms of anxiety, depression, and stress. For example, a meta-analysis published in the Journal of the American Medical Association (JAMA) found that mindfulness meditation interventions were moderately effective in reducing symptoms of anxiety, depression, and pain. Another study published in the journal Psychiatry Research showed that mindfulness meditation was associated with significant reductions in symptoms of depression and anxiety among individuals with mood disorders.

Creative expression, whether through art, music, or writing, fosters self-expression and creativity, unlocking new insights and perspectives. Engaging in creative expression, whether through art, music, writing, or other forms, has been shown to have therapeutic benefits for mental health and well-being. A study published in the Journal of Positive Psychology found that engaging in creative activities, such as painting or writing, was associated with increased positive emotions and decreased negative emotions. Research published in the Journal of Art Therapy demonstrated that art therapy interventions were effective in reducing symptoms of anxiety, depression, and stress among individuals with various mental health conditions.

Gratitude rituals, such as daily gratitude journaling or mindfulness practices, cultivate appreciation and positivity, shifting focus from challenges to blessings. By experimenting with these transformative practices, individuals can discover which resonate most with them and incorporate them into their daily routines. Research on gratitude journaling has consistently shown its positive impact on well-being. Gratitude journaling involves regularly writing down things for which one is grateful, fostering a sense of appreciation and resilience. A study published in the Journal of Personality and Social Psychology found that participants who kept gratitude journals reported higher levels of subjective well-being and lower levels of negative emotions compared to those who did not. Additionally, research published in the Journal of Happiness Studies revealed that gratitude journaling was associated with increased feelings of happiness and life satisfaction, as well as reduced symptoms of depression.

Practical Exercise:

Experiment with different transformative practices such as journaling, creative expression, or gratitude rituals, and observe how they impact your mindset and outlook. Transformative practices come in many forms, each offering unique benefits for personal development. Journaling, for example, provides a space for self-reflection and emotional processing, allowing individuals to explore their thoughts, feelings, and experiences in a structured manner.

Reflection Prompt:

Which transformative practices resonate most with you, and how can you incorporate them into your daily life? Reflecting on the transformative practices that resonate most with you allows for deeper introspection and intentionality in integrating them into your daily life. Consider which practices align with your values, interests, and personal goals. Are you drawn to journaling as a means of self-expression and reflection? Do you find solace and inspiration in creative pursuits such as painting, playing music, or writing poetry? Or perhaps you feel a sense of peace and contentment when practicing gratitude and mindfulness rituals. Once you identify the transformative practices that resonate most with you, brainstorm practical ways to incorporate them into your daily routine. Whether it's setting aside dedicated time each day for journaling, scheduling regular creative sessions, or integrating mindfulness exercises into your morning routine, find what works best for you and commit to nurturing these practices as pathways to personal growth and fulfillment.

Transformative practices offer a pathway to self-discovery, empowerment, and growth. By engaging in practices that nourish the mind, body, and spirit, individuals can cultivate a deeper sense of purpose, resilience, and well-being. Experimenting with different transformative practices and reflecting on their impact allows for continuous growth and evolution on the journey toward personal fulfillment. As you embark on this transformative journey, embrace curiosity, openness, and self-compassion, knowing that each practice holds the potential to unlock new insights, expand awareness, and inspire profound transformation.

Transitioning from the exploration of transformative practices, I also draw from my experiences as a consultant alongside my husband, where we've witnessed firsthand the profound impact of these methods on our clients. While maintaining confidentiality, I've been granted permission to share case studies showcasing how transformative practices have helped individuals on their journey of self-transformation.

Case Study 1: Michelle's Journey to Confidence

Michelle, a single mother of seven and a high-level executive, reached out to our consulting firm at a pivotal moment in her life. Despite her successful career in the corporate world, Michelle felt a deep longing to pursue her entrepreneurial dreams in the beauty industry. Uncertain whether to start with private labeling skincare products or opening a beauty supply store, Michelle was overwhelmed by the magnitude of the decision ahead of her.

As an army veteran and a black woman with five successful businesses, including two beauty supply stores, I resonated with Michelle's journey on a personal level. I understood the weight of her aspirations and the challenges she faced as she navigated the transition from corporate life to entrepreneurship. With empathy and understanding, I welcomed Michelle into our coaching program, determined to support her every step of the way.

During our initial conversations, Michelle shared her fears and uncertainties, expressing her desire to find clarity and confidence in her entrepreneurial path. Together, we explored mindfulness techniques and self-reflection exercises to help Michelle uncover her inner strengths and values. Through guided meditation and deep introspection, Michelle began to peel back the layers of self-doubt and insecurity that had held her back for so long.

As Michelle immersed herself in the transformative practices we provided, she experienced a profound shift in perspective. She discovered a newfound sense of resilience and determination, drawing inspiration from her own journey and the success stories of others. With each session, Michelle's confidence grew, fueled by the unwavering support and guidance of our coaching team.

Michelle's journey was not without its challenges. There were moments of doubt and uncertainty, but she persevered, drawing strength from her newfound sense of purpose. With each obstacle she overcame, Michelle emerged stronger and more determined than ever before.

As Michelle reflected on her journey, she realized that her entrepreneurial path was not just about building a business—it was about reclaiming her sense of purpose and identity. With newfound clarity, Michelle made the courageous decision to pursue her passion for beauty entrepreneurship, starting with the launch of her own skincare line.

Today, Michelle stands tall as a shining example of courage and resilience. She has embraced her role as an entrepreneur with grace and determination, inspiring others with her unwavering commitment to success. Through her transformational journey, Sarah has not only achieved her dreams but has also become a beacon of hope and inspiration for those who dare to pursue their passions against all odds.

Case Study 2: *John's Journey of Rediscovery*

John, a devoted husband and father, found himself at a crossroads in his life. After being unexpectedly let go from his position as a software engineer, he embarked on a new chapter in the real estate field. However, amidst this transition, John grappled with feelings of uncertainty and self-doubt. He questioned whether he was truly following his "why" in life and struggled to find fulfillment in his new career path.

In addition to the challenges of his professional transition, John found himself battling a profound sense of depression. The weight of uncertainty and the fear of failure weighed heavily on his shoulders, casting a shadow over his once-vibrant spirit. It was in this state of darkness that John turned to transformative practices as a beacon of hope and healing.

Incorporating creative expression into his daily routine, John sought refuge in activities such as painting and photography. Despite initial skepticism and hesitancy, he soon discovered that these creative outlets offered him a sanctuary from the chaos of his mind. With each brushstroke and click of the shutter, John found solace and release, allowing his innermost emotions to flow freely onto the canvas and through the lens of his camera.

As John delved deeper into his creative pursuits, he began to experience a profound shift in perspective. The act of creation became a form of therapy, a means of untangling the knots of his tangled thoughts and emotions. Through his art, John found a voice he never knew he possessed—a voice that spoke volumes without uttering a single word.

In the midst of his struggles, John's creativity emerged as a guiding light, illuminating a path of rediscovery and renewal. His journey of self-expression not only brought him joy and fulfillment but also rekindled a sense of purpose and passion within him. With each painting and photograph, John found himself inching closer to the truth of his "why" in life, realizing that it was not merely a destination but a journey of exploration and self-discovery.

Today, John stands as a testament to the transformative power of creative expression in overcoming adversity and finding meaning in the midst of chaos. Through his journey, he has not only embraced his inner artist but has also rediscovered the essence of his being. As he continues to navigate the ups and downs of life's journey, John serves as an inspiration to others, reminding us all that the darkest of nights can give birth to the brightest of stars.

Case Study 3: *Emily's Journey to Gratitude*

Emily, a driven entrepreneur juggling the demands of her business and personal life, found herself caught in a relentless cycle of busyness and overwhelm. Despite her success in the business world, Emily struggled to find balance and fulfillment amidst the constant demands on her time and energy. As the weight of her responsibilities grew heavier, Emily yearned for a sense of peace and equilibrium in her life.

Introducing gratitude rituals into her daily routine, Emily embarked on a journey of self-discovery and transformation. Recognizing the need to prioritize her well-being amidst the chaos of her schedule, Emily began journaling about moments of appreciation and practicing mindfulness exercises to anchor herself in the present moment. With each entry in her gratitude journal and each mindful breath she took, Emily found herself inching closer to a state of inner harmony and contentment.

As Emily immersed herself in these transformative practices, she experienced a profound shift in perspective. The simple act of expressing gratitude for the blessings in her life opened her eyes to the abundance that surrounded her, from the laughter of loved ones to the beauty of nature. Through mindfulness exercises, Emily learned to quiet the noise of her mind and tune into the richness of the present moment, finding joy in the little things that had previously gone unnoticed.

As a result of her dedication to gratitude rituals and mindfulness practices, Emily discovered a newfound sense of balance and fulfillment in her relationships and work. She approached each day with a renewed sense of purpose and appreciation, infusing her interactions with authenticity and presence. In the midst of her busy schedule, Emily found moments of serenity and connection that nourished her soul and replenished her spirit.

Today, Emily stands as a shining example of the transformative power of gratitude and mindfulness in cultivating inner peace and fulfillment. Through her journey, she has not only found balance amidst the chaos but has also rediscovered the joy of living fully in the present moment. As she continues to navigate the twists and turns of her entrepreneurial journey, Emily serves as an inspiration to others, reminding us all of the profound impact that gratitude and mindfulness can have on our lives.

These case studies highlight the transformative power of mindfulness, creativity, and gratitude in fostering personal growth and fulfillment. Through these practices, individuals like Sarah, John, and Emily have unlocked their potential, overcome obstacles, and embraced the journey of self-transformation with courage and resilience.

Cultivating Positive Relationships

Cultivating Positive Relationships is a crucial aspect of personal growth, as social connections profoundly influence our experiences and outlook. Research consistently highlights the positive impact of strong social ties on well-being, happiness, and overall life satisfaction. These relationships provide crucial support during difficult times, opportunities for meaningful connections, and a sense of belonging. Whether with family, friends, colleagues, or romantic partners, investing in nurturing relationships enriches our lives and enhances our journey of personal development.

From understanding the significance of social connections, let's explore strategies for fostering healthy relationships. Building and maintaining healthy relationships require active effort, empathy, and effective communication. It entails genuinely listening to others, demonstrating compassion and understanding, and prioritizing mutual respect and trust. By cultivating qualities like empathy, kindness, and patience, we create a positive environment where relationships can thrive. Moreover, expressing gratitude and appreciation for those in our lives strengthens bonds and fosters a deeper sense of connection and reciprocity.

Establishing boundaries is essential for preserving healthy relationships and safeguarding our well-being. Boundaries delineate acceptable behaviors, expectations, and limits within relationships, fostering a sense of safety and respect. Effective communication is vital in setting boundaries assertively and respectfully, ensuring that our needs and values are respected. By clearly communicating our boundaries and addressing conflicts or misunderstandings promptly, we foster healthier and more fulfilling relationships based on mutual understanding and respect.

Moving from setting boundaries, let's highlight the importance of practicing effective communication in nurturing positive relationships. Effective communication serves as the foundation of healthy relationships, enabling individuals to express their thoughts, feelings, and needs openly and honestly. It involves active listening, empathy, and non-judgmental communication, fostering understanding and connection between individuals. By honing skills such as active listening, expressing empathy, and using "I" statements, we can navigate conflicts, resolve misunderstandings, and strengthen our relationships.

Cultivating positive relationships is an ongoing process that demands intentionality, effort, and vulnerability. Recognizing the profound impact of social connections on personal growth and implementing strategies for fostering healthy relationships, setting boundaries, and practicing effective communication empower us to cultivate fulfilling connections that support our well-being and contribute to our overall happiness and fulfillment in life.

Overcoming common challenges in relationships is essential for fostering healthy connections and strengthening bonds with loved ones. Conflict resolution, managing differences, and navigating transitions are all integral aspects of building resilient relationships that can withstand the tests of time and adversity. In my own family, we've faced significant challenges in our relationships with our parents. These challenges stemmed from past grievances and misunderstandings that strained our connections over the years. However, as time went on, we began to recognize the importance of overcoming these obstacles and rebuilding our relationships.

One pivotal moment occurred when my father fell ill with COVID-19. Despite the strained relationships between my siblings and me, and our father, we rallied together in his time of need. Prompted by my older sister, who maintained a closer relationship with him, we set aside our differences and united to support him. Throughout his illness, we maintained constant communication, offering words of encouragement and ensuring he received the care he needed. As my father recovered and was released from the hospital, it provided an opportunity for us to start anew and rebuild our relationship with him.

Reflecting on my father brings to mind memories of mental manipulation, abuse, and constant fear experienced during my childhood. For a long time, these memories were difficult to shake off. My mother often remarked on my resemblance to him, inadvertently instilling in me a fear of inheriting his negative traits. Although she meant it in jest, the impact on me was profound, and I harbored a deep-seated apprehension about becoming like him. Despite the challenges of overcoming such a childhood, with prayer, concerted effort, and love, we endeavored to move forward to the best of our abilities. While I can't speak for my siblings, I find solace in where we stand today. We have forged a better understanding and relationship, marked by growth and healing.

Despite the hurdles, this experience served as a catalyst for positive change and reconciliation within our family. Today, my father has established a strong bond with my children, showcasing his capacity for growth and transformation over time.

Navigating relationships with my mother has presented its own set of challenges, particularly as my brother and I maintain more distant connections with her compared to my older sister. However, through these challenges, I've come to realize that finding inner peace doesn't necessarily hinge on changing others; rather, it involves accepting people as they are, flaws and all, while nurturing love in its unique form. Alongside these personal reflections, my journey to becoming a psychologist has offered insights into my mother's experiences from a systems perspective, shedding light on the intergenerational transmission of trauma. As one of sixteen children, my mother's upbringing was marked by a constant struggle for love and attention, with little opportunity for therapeutic intervention. Unknowingly, she perpetuates the cycle of inherited trauma, passing down unresolved issues from past generations.

Scientifically speaking, the transmission of trauma across generations can be understood through the concept of epigenetics. During prenatal development, the environment experienced by an individual, including their mother's experiences, can influence the expression of genes. This means that the stress and trauma experienced by previous generations can leave biological marks on DNA, which may impact the emotional and psychological well-being of offspring. Furthermore, research suggests that traumatic experiences can alter the development of sperm and eggs, potentially passing on genetic changes to future generations. Therefore, many of the challenges we face in life may stem from inherited trauma that predates our existence.

As I've learned to forgive and move forward, I've recognized the importance of accountability, particularly within the family unit. My mother's inability to hold others accountable reflects her own upbringing, highlighting the profound impact of generational patterns on familial dynamics. This realization underscores the need for compassionate understanding and a commitment to breaking the cycle of inherited trauma through awareness and intervention. Despite the challenges and negative experiences that occurred, I wouldn't alter anything about my upbringing because it has shaped me into the person I am today. By the age of ten, I had shared dinner tables with senators, politicians, and global leaders. I had been featured in newspapers and emerged as a young activist, marching and protesting in Albany, the state capital, for justice, notably in the case of Amadou Diallo. I vividly recall being photographed for a newspaper, holding a sign declaring, "I missed school today to fight for justice for Amadou Diallo," and passionately discussing my beliefs in interviews. My mother wasn't much of a traveler back then but she instilled in us an appreciation for the finer aspects of life in New York City, taking us on adventures throughout the city. Her radiant smile and lively dance moves illuminated every family gathering, while my father's infectious laughter and culinary skills added joy to every cookout. Despite its challenges, I am deeply grateful for my upbringing and the valuable lessons it has imparted as I navigate adulthood.

Conflict resolution is an inevitable aspect of any relationship, whether it's with family members, friends, colleagues, or romantic partners. However, how we approach and navigate conflicts can significantly impact the health and longevity of our relationships. One effective strategy for resolving conflicts is to practice active listening and empathy. Instead of focusing solely on getting our point across, take the time to listen to the other person's perspective with an open mind and genuine empathy. Reflecting back what you've heard and validating the other person's feelings can help foster understanding and pave the way for finding mutually acceptable solutions. I've found that active listening and empathy are invaluable tools for fostering understanding and finding common ground. By truly listening to the perspectives of others and empathizing with their feelings, we can build bridges of communication and mutual respect. Instead of focusing solely on proving our point, let's prioritize understanding and validation. Let's remember that conflicts often arise from differences in values, beliefs, or personalities. It's essential to approach these differences with curiosity and a willingness to learn from each other, recognizing that diversity enriches our relationships. Through open dialogue, empathy, and a commitment to finding common ground, we can navigate conflicts and differences with grace and understanding.

Transitioning into another key aspect of conflict resolution, maintaining a calm and respectful demeanor, even in the heat of the moment, is crucial. Avoid resorting to personal attacks or blame, and instead, focus on addressing the issue at hand constructively. Using "I" statements to express your thoughts and feelings can help prevent defensiveness and promote productive dialogue. For example, instead of saying, "You never listen to me," try saying, "I feel frustrated when I don't feel heard." Conflicts inevitably arise in relationships, but how we approach and navigate them can profoundly impact their health and longevity. One effective strategy is active listening and empathy, wherein we genuinely listen to the other person's perspective and validate their feelings. This fosters understanding and paves the way for mutually acceptable solutions. Maintaining a calm and respectful demeanor, even in heated moments, is crucial. We should avoid personal attacks and focus on addressing the issue constructively. By using "I" statements and seeking common ground, we can resolve conflicts collaboratively, prioritizing the relationship's well-being over winning.

Moving forward, it's essential to be willing to compromise and seek common ground when resolving conflicts. Instead of approaching conflicts with a win-lose mentality, strive for solutions that meet the needs and interests of both parties involved. Brainstorming potential solutions together and exploring creative alternatives can help find mutually beneficial outcomes that strengthen the relationship rather than erode it.

Navigating differences in relationships, whether they stem from values, beliefs, or personalities, poses a common challenge. While these differences can enhance relationships by introducing diversity and fresh perspectives, they may also spark misunderstandings and conflicts if not handled thoughtfully. An effective approach to managing differences involves practicing empathy and striving to understand the other person's perspective without judgment or criticism. It's important to acknowledge that disagreements are natural and acceptable within any relationship. Addressing differences openly and respectfully is crucial. By creating a safe environment for open dialogue, where both parties feel free to express their thoughts and feelings without fear of judgment, we foster understanding and respect. The key lies in finding common ground and seeking compromise through mutual understanding. Embracing and managing differences are fundamental to nurturing healthy relationships. By openly recognizing and addressing disparities in values, beliefs, or personalities, we create an atmosphere conducive to understanding and mutual respect. Through active listening and open communication, we gain valuable insights into each other's viewpoints and identify areas of agreement.

Approaching differences with curiosity and a willingness to learn from one another, rather than as barriers, allows us to celebrate our individuality and engage in respectful discourse. By doing so, we not only navigate differences gracefully but also deepen our connections with those we hold dear. Differences in values, beliefs, or personalities are common in relationships and can either enrich or strain them. Practicing empathy and understanding the other person's perspective without judgment is key to managing differences effectively. We should create a safe space for open dialogue, where both parties feel free to express their thoughts and feelings without fear of reprisal. Embracing and addressing differences openly fosters understanding and respect, allowing us to celebrate diversity and deepen our connections. Approaching differences with curiosity and a willingness to learn from each other enriches our relationships and enhances our growth together.

Furthermore, approaching differences with curiosity and a willingness to learn from each other is essential. Instead of viewing differences as obstacles, see them as opportunities for growth and enrichment. Embrace diversity and celebrate the unique qualities that each person brings to the relationship, recognizing that it's our differences that make us stronger together. Transitioning into navigating transitions in relationships, such as moving in together or starting a family, presents challenges that require careful navigation. These transitions often involve significant changes in roles, responsibilities, and dynamics, which can strain relationships if not managed effectively. One effective strategy for navigating transitions is to approach them with open communication and collaboration.

It is very important to be patient and flexible during periods of transition, recognizing that adjustment takes time and effort. Be prepared to adapt and make compromises as needed, and prioritize maintaining connection and support throughout the process. Lean on each other for emotional support and encouragement, and celebrate milestones and achievements together as you navigate the transition as a team. Cultivating positive relationships requires intentionality, effort, and a willingness to navigate challenges with grace and compassion. By practicing effective conflict resolution, managing differences with empathy and respect, and navigating transitions collaboratively, we can strengthen our connections and foster deeper bonds with those we care about. Remember that relationships are a journey, and it's the shared experiences and challenges we overcome together that ultimately deepen our connections and enrich our lives.

Reflecting on the journey through this chapter, I'm reminded of the profound impact that positive relationships can have on our lives. From understanding the importance of social connections to navigating conflicts and managing differences, each insight serves as a guiding light on our path to cultivating fulfilling relationships. As we conclude, I encourage you to take a moment to reflect on how these strategies resonate with your own experiences and relationships. How can you apply active listening, empathy, and effective communication in your interactions? What boundaries do you need to set to safeguard your well-being while nurturing meaningful connections? By integrating these practices into your daily life, you have the power to enrich your relationships and foster deeper bonds with those who matter most. Remember, it's the shared journey of growth and understanding that ultimately strengthens our connections and enhances our lives.

Practical Exercise:

1. *Reach out to a friend or loved one and express gratitude for their presence in your life. Practice active listening and empathy during your conversation.*

Reflection Prompt:

1. *How do positive relationships contribute to your sense of fulfillment and well-being?*

Overcoming Obstacles

Life is a journey filled with twists, turns, and unexpected hurdles that can often leave us feeling overwhelmed and uncertain. In Chapter 8, we delve into the intricate landscape of overcoming obstacles, exploring the myriad strategies and approaches that can empower us to not just navigate challenges, but to emerge stronger and more resilient than before. From the inevitable setbacks that punctuate our paths to the daunting task of confronting our deepest fears, each obstacle presents an opportunity for growth and self-discovery. By embarking on this exploration together, we uncover the transformative power of resilience and determination, illuminating the path forward towards personal fulfillment and success. Through a nuanced exploration of proven coping mechanisms and invaluable insights, we equip ourselves with the tools needed to navigate life's inevitable hurdles with grace and resilience. Join us on this transformative journey as we uncover the keys to overcoming adversity and thriving in the face of life's greatest challenges.

Adversity comes in myriad forms, ranging from the personal setbacks that test our resolve to the external challenges thrust upon us by the unpredictability of life itself. It's in these moments of trial and tribulation that we are truly tested, our resilience and determination put to the ultimate test. Yet, amidst the chaos and uncertainty, it's imperative to recognize that adversity is not merely a roadblock on our journey; rather, it serves as a catalyst for profound personal growth and development. By reframing our perspective and embracing a mindset of resilience, we transform obstacles into opportunities for learning and self-discovery. Through the crucible of adversity, we uncover hidden strengths, unearth dormant talents, and forge deeper connections with ourselves and the world around us. Each challenge becomes a stepping stone on the path to self-actualization, guiding us towards a more profound understanding of who we are and who we are destined to become. Embracing adversity with courage and determination, we navigate the turbulent waters of life with unwavering grace and resilience, emerging stronger and more resilient with each passing storm.

Resilience, often described as the essence of inner strength, goes beyond simply enduring hardships; it's about bouncing back from setbacks with newfound determination. At its core, resilience involves nurturing our inner fortitude, adapting to challenges, and maintaining a positive outlook despite adversity. In the realm of resilience, we encounter a wealth of strategies and practices that empower us to navigate life's challenges with grace and resilience. At the heart of this journey lies the practice of self-care, a fundamental aspect that underpins resilience. By prioritizing activities like adequate rest, nourishing nutrition, regular exercise, and moments of relaxation, we replenish our physical, mental, and emotional well-being. These acts of self-care serve as a shield, fortifying us against the onslaught of stress and adversity, enabling us to face challenges with renewed strength and resilience.

Fear is a natural response to the unknown, but it can also hold us back from reaching our full potential. In this section, we will discuss techniques for confronting and overcoming fears, including gradual exposure, cognitive restructuring, and mindfulness practices. By facing our fears head-on, we can expand our comfort zones and unlock new possibilities for growth and achievement. Fear is something we all grapple with—it's a natural reaction to the unknown, a feeling that can either protect us or hold us back. In this part of our journey, we'll dive into the realm of fear, exploring how it impacts our lives and discovering ways to confront and overcome it. By getting to know fear on a personal level and learning how to navigate its twists and turns, we can open doors to growth and self-discovery we never thought possible.

Confronting our fears isn't easy—it takes courage and determination. One approach we'll explore is gradual exposure, where we take small steps to face our fears in a safe and controlled manner. Each step forward helps us build confidence and resilience, slowly chipping away at the walls fear builds around us. Another powerful tool in our kit is cognitive restructuring, where we challenge the negative thoughts and beliefs that fuel our fears. By reshaping our perspective and reframing our fears, we can reclaim control over our lives and rewrite our narratives. And then there's mindfulness—a practice that invites us to embrace the present moment with open arms. Through mindfulness, we learn to observe our fears without judgment, allowing them to exist without letting them consume us. By tuning into our breath, practicing meditation, and grounding ourselves in the here and now, we create space to confront our fears with courage and compassion. It's through these practices that we can expand our comfort zones, embrace new possibilities, and step into our true potential, one fearless moment at a time.

Change is inevitable, but it can be challenging to navigate, especially when it's unexpected or unwanted. Embracing change can be a daunting prospect, as it often entails stepping into the unknown and relinquishing the familiar comforts of the past. However, change is an inevitable part of life, and learning to adapt is crucial for personal growth and resilience. In this section, we'll explore strategies for navigating change with grace and resilience, empowering us to embrace new opportunities and navigate transitions with confidence.

One key strategy for adapting to change is practicing acceptance. Rather than resisting or denying change, acceptance involves acknowledging and embracing it as an inevitable aspect of life. By accepting the reality of change, we free ourselves from the grip of fear and uncertainty, allowing us to move forward with greater ease and clarity. Acceptance doesn't mean passively resigning ourselves to circumstances; instead, it empowers us to make peace with the present moment and approach change with an open heart and mind. Maintaining flexibility is another essential skill for navigating change effectively. Flexibility involves remaining open to new possibilities and adjusting our plans and expectations as circumstances evolve. By cultivating a flexible mindset, we can adapt to changing circumstances with agility and resilience, rather than becoming overwhelmed or paralyzed by uncertainty. Flexibility allows us to embrace the fluidity of life, responding to challenges with creativity and resourcefulness.

Seeking opportunities for growth is a mindset shift that can transform how we approach change. Instead of viewing change as a threat or inconvenience, we can choose to see it as an opportunity for personal and professional development. By seeking out opportunities for growth within change, we can harness its transformative potential and emerge stronger, wiser, and more resilient. Whether it's learning new skills, embracing new experiences, or stepping outside our comfort zones, embracing change as a catalyst for growth empowers us to thrive in the face of uncertainty. By practicing acceptance, maintaining flexibility, and seeking opportunities for growth, we can navigate change with grace and resilience. Embracing change as a natural part of life allows us to approach transitions with openness and curiosity, rather than fear and resistance. As we cultivate these strategies, we empower ourselves to embrace the ever-changing landscape of life with confidence, adaptability, and a sense of possibility.

Setbacks are a natural part of any journey, but they can also be opportunities for growth and learning. By adopting a growth mindset and focusing on solutions rather than dwelling on problems, we can transform setbacks into opportunities for personal and professional development. When setbacks hit, it's easy to feel defeated and overwhelmed. But what if we could see them as stepping stones instead of stumbling blocks? It's all about shifting our perspective and finding the silver lining in the clouds. One way to do this is by looking at setbacks as opportunities for growth and learning. Rather than dwelling on what went wrong, we can focus on the lessons we've gained and how they can guide us forward. It's like turning lemons into lemonade—taking the sour moments and transforming them into something sweet. And it's not just about bouncing back; it's about bouncing forward, stronger and wiser than before. With a mindset of growth and resilience, setbacks become not roadblocks but milestones on the path to success.

Overcoming obstacles is an essential skill for navigating life's challenges and achieving our goals. By cultivating resilience, facing fears, navigating change, and turning setbacks into opportunities, we can overcome adversity and thrive in any situation. Remember that challenges are opportunities in disguise, and with the right mindset and strategies, we can overcome any obstacle that comes our way. Embarking on a journey of self-transformation is a powerful endeavor, yet it's not without its challenges.

Embarking on a journey of self-transformation can be both exhilarating and daunting. Along the way, we often encounter common barriers that hinder our progress and challenge our resolve. One such barrier is the fear of failure, which can paralyze us and prevent us from taking risks or pursuing our goals. The fear of failure stems from a deep-seated aversion to disappointment and rejection, causing us to play it safe and stick to the familiar rather than venture into the unknown. To overcome this barrier, it's essential to reframe failure as a natural part of the learning process and embrace it as an opportunity for growth. By shifting our mindset and viewing failure as feedback rather than a reflection of our worth, we can cultivate resilience and courageously pursue our aspirations.

Another common barrier to self-transformation is self-doubt, which can undermine our confidence and sabotage our efforts to change. Self-doubt often manifests as negative self-talk and a lack of belief in our abilities, leading us to second-guess ourselves and question our worthiness. To overcome self-doubt, it's important to practice self-compassion and challenge the negative beliefs that fuel it. By acknowledging our fears and insecurities with kindness and understanding, we can begin to cultivate self-confidence and trust in ourselves. Additionally, surrounding ourselves with supportive individuals who believe in our potential can provide encouragement and validation, bolstering our confidence and helping us overcome self-doubt.

Comfort zones can be another significant barrier to self-transformation, as they represent familiarity and security, making change feel uncomfortable and intimidating. Stepping outside our comfort zones requires us to confront uncertainty and face the unknown, triggering feelings of anxiety and resistance. However, growth often lies beyond the boundaries of our comfort zones, necessitating a willingness to embrace discomfort and take calculated risks. To overcome this barrier, it's essential to adopt a gradual approach and ease into new experiences gradually. By setting small, manageable goals and gradually expanding our comfort zones, we can build confidence and resilience over time. Additionally, cultivating a growth mindset, which emphasizes the belief that our abilities can be developed through effort and perseverance, can empower us to embrace challenges as opportunities for growth rather than threats to our security.

A lack of support can hinder our journey of self-transformation, leaving us feeling isolated and overwhelmed. Whether it's a lack of encouragement from friends and family or a dearth of resources and guidance, navigating transformation alone can be daunting. To overcome this barrier, it's crucial to seek out supportive communities, mentors, or professional guidance that can provide encouragement, accountability, and practical advice. By surrounding ourselves with individuals who believe in our potential and offer guidance and support, we can overcome obstacles and achieve our goals more effectively. Additionally, fostering connections with like-minded individuals who share similar aspirations can provide a sense of camaraderie and solidarity, making the journey of self-transformation feel less daunting and more rewarding. Understanding these obstacles and equipping ourselves with the right tools and mindset, we can navigate the path to personal growth with greater clarity and resilience.

Identifying Common Barriers:

1. Fear of Failure: One of the most common barriers to self-transformation is the fear of failure. This fear can paralyze us, preventing us from taking risks and pursuing our goals. To overcome this barrier, it's essential to reframe failure as a natural part of the learning process and to cultivate resilience in the face of setbacks.

2. Self-Doubt: Doubting ourselves and our abilities can undermine our confidence and motivation to change. To overcome self-doubt, it's important to practice self-compassion, challenge negative self-talk, and focus on our strengths and accomplishments.

3. Comfort Zone: Stepping outside of our comfort zone can be uncomfortable and intimidating, leading many to resist change. However, growth often lies beyond our comfort zone. To overcome this barrier, we must embrace discomfort as a sign of growth and gradually expand our comfort zone through small, manageable steps.

4. Lack of Support: Surrounding ourselves with supportive individuals can greatly enhance our journey of self-transformation. However, some may lack the support they need from friends, family, or colleagues. To overcome this barrier, seek out supportive communities, mentors, or professional guidance to provide encouragement and accountability.

5. Perfectionism: Striving for perfection can create unrealistic expectations and lead to feelings of inadequacy. To overcome perfectionism, it's important to embrace imperfection, focus on progress rather than perfection, and celebrate small victories along the way.

Strategies for Overcoming Barriers:

1. Cultivate Self-Compassion: Practice self-compassion by treating yourself with kindness and understanding, especially in times of difficulty or failure. Recognize that everyone faces obstacles on their journey, and offer yourself the same empathy and support you would give to a friend.

2. Set Realistic Goals: Break down your transformational goals into smaller, manageable steps and set realistic timelines for achieving them. By focusing on incremental progress, you can build momentum and maintain motivation throughout your journey.

3. Seek Support: Surround yourself with a supportive network of friends, family, mentors, or professionals who can provide encouragement, guidance, and accountability. Share your goals and challenges openly with others and lean on them for support when needed.

4. Challenge Negative Beliefs: Identify and challenge any negative beliefs or self-limiting beliefs that may be holding you back. Replace these beliefs with positive affirmations and empowering thoughts that reinforce your worth and potential for growth.

5. Embrace Failure as a Learning Opportunity: Reframe failure as a natural and necessary part of the learning process. Instead of viewing setbacks as evidence of inadequacy, see them as valuable learning opportunities that can propel you forward on your journey of self-transformation.

    Overcoming barriers to self-transformation requires courage, resilience, and a willingness to confront our fears and limitations. By identifying common barriers such as fear of failure, self-doubt, comfort zone, lack of support, and perfectionism, and implementing strategies like cultivating self-compassion, setting realistic goals, seeking support, challenging negative beliefs, and embracing failure as a learning opportunity, we can navigate the path to personal growth with greater clarity and resilience. Remember that transformation is a journey, and every obstacle we overcome brings us closer to becoming the best version of ourselves. Dealing with setbacks requires a resilient mindset and a proactive approach. When faced with obstacles or failures, it's crucial to acknowledge and process the accompanying emotions while reframing setbacks as opportunities for growth. Reflecting on the lessons learned from setbacks enables individuals to adjust their strategies, refine their goals, and cultivate resilience. By embracing setbacks as integral parts of the journey rather than indicators of failure, individuals can harness their inner strength to persevere and ultimately thrive despite challenges.

    Managing self-doubt involves challenging negative thoughts and beliefs while nurturing self-compassion and confidence. When self-doubt arises, individuals can counter it by focusing on their strengths, achievements, and past successes. Setting realistic expectations and seeking external validation from supportive sources can provide reassurance and perspective. Additionally, practicing self-compassion and treating oneself with kindness during moments of doubt fosters resilience and a sense of self-worth. By cultivating a positive self-image and embracing personal growth, individuals can navigate self-doubt with greater clarity and confidence on their journey towards self-fulfillment.

Dealing with setbacks and managing self-doubt are two significant challenges on the path to self-transformation. Here's how to address them effectively:

1. **Dealing with Setbacks:**

- Acknowledge Your Feelings: Allow yourself to feel disappointed or frustrated when setbacks occur. It's natural to experience negative emotions, but try not to dwell on them for too long.

-Reflect and Learn: Instead of viewing setbacks as failures, see them as opportunities for growth and learning. Reflect on what went wrong and what you can do differently next time.

-Adjust Your Approach: Use setbacks as valuable feedback to refine your goals and strategies. Adapt your approach based on the lessons learned from the setback to increase your chances of success in the future.

-Practice Resilience: Cultivate resilience by reminding yourself of past successes and your ability to overcome challenges. Trust in your capacity to bounce back and persevere in the face of adversity.

2. **Managing Self-Doubt:**

-Challenge Negative Thoughts: When self-doubt creeps in, challenge negative thoughts and beliefs about yourself. Replace them with positive affirmations and evidence of your past achievements and capabilities.

-Focus on Strengths: Shift your focus from your perceived weaknesses to your strengths and accomplishments. Recognize your unique talents and qualities that contribute to your success.

-Set Realistic Expectations: Avoid setting unrealistic expectations for yourself, as they can fuel self-doubt. Set achievable goals and celebrate small victories along the way to build confidence and momentum.

-Seek External Validation: Seek feedback and validation from trusted friends, mentors, or colleagues who can provide objective perspectives on your abilities and achievements.

-Practice Self-Compassion: Be kind to yourself and treat yourself with the same compassion and understanding you would offer to a friend facing self-doubt. Acknowledge that everyone experiences moments of doubt and that it's a normal part of the human experience.

By implementing these strategies, you can effectively deal with setbacks and manage self-doubt on your journey of self-transformation. Remember that transformation is a process, and setbacks and doubts are merely temporary obstacles that can be overcome with resilience, perseverance, and self-belief. Seeking support from mentors, coaches, or therapists can be incredibly beneficial on the journey of self-transformation and personal growth. Mentors and coaches offer guidance, wisdom, and perspective gained from their own experiences, helping individuals navigate challenges and make informed decisions. They provide encouragement, accountability, and practical advice to help individuals overcome obstacles and achieve their goals. Therapists, on the other hand, offer a safe and confidential space for individuals to explore their thoughts, emotions, and behaviors. They provide therapeutic techniques and interventions to address underlying issues, improve coping skills, and promote emotional well-being.

Despite the undeniable benefits of therapy, there are often contradictions towards it, particularly within the black community. Historical and systemic factors, such as stigma, mistrust, and cultural barriers, contribute to these contradictions. Stigma surrounding mental health and therapy persists due to societal misconceptions and negative stereotypes, leading many to view seeking help as a sign of weakness or failure. Mistrust towards mental health professionals can stem from historical abuses and disparities in healthcare, perpetuating skepticism and reluctance to seek support. Additionally, cultural norms and values within the black community, such as strength, resilience, and self-reliance, may discourage individuals from acknowledging their mental health struggles or seeking external assistance. However, addressing these contradictions requires destigmatizing mental health, promoting culturally competent care, and encouraging open dialogue about the importance of seeking support for emotional well-being within the black community. By recognizing the value of therapy and embracing culturally sensitive approaches to mental health care, individuals can overcome barriers to seeking support and access the resources they need to thrive.

Therapy emerges as a remarkable option because of its fundamental quality: the therapist's impartiality and lack of personal connection with you. This aspect allows for a refreshing openness and honesty, unhampered by the usual considerations of social dynamics or personal relationships. It's like having a trusted confidant who is solely there to listen, support, and guide you through life's challenges without any preconceived notions or biases. The sense of anonymity and confidentiality in therapy creates a safe haven where you can freely explore your innermost thoughts, fears, and struggles. Knowing that your privacy is respected enables you to delve into sensitive issues with confidence, knowing that you won't face judgment or consequences for your honesty. In this space, therapists offer validation, understanding, and practical tools for navigating life's ups and downs with resilience and grace. Through this process, you can find clarity, healing, and empowerment to navigate life's challenges and embrace your full potential. So, consider therapy not just as a resource for mental health, but as a pathway to self-discovery, growth, and fulfillment, guided by the compassionate presence of a dedicated therapist.

As we close out Chapter 8, here are some interactive exercises and reflection prompts that invite you to engage more deeply with the strategies discussed. These exercises are designed to help you apply the concepts to your own life, cultivate resilience, confront fears, expand your comfort zone, and set actionable goals for personal growth. By taking the time to reflect on these prompts and actively participate in the exercises, you can gain greater insight into overcoming obstacles and thriving in the face of adversity. Remember, transformation is a journey, and every step you take towards self-discovery and growth brings you closer to becoming the best version of yourself.

1. *Resilience Inventory:*

    - *Reflect on past experiences where you have overcome obstacles or setbacks. Write down three instances where you demonstrated resilience.*
    - *Identify the strengths and coping strategies you utilized in each situation. How did these strengths and strategies contribute to your ability to bounce back from adversity?*
    - *Consider how you can apply these strengths and strategies to current challenges or obstacles you are facing. Write down*

actionable steps you can take to cultivate resilience in your daily life.

2. ***Fear Exploration:***

- *Identify a fear or limiting belief that is holding you back from reaching your goals or pursuing your dreams.*
- *Reflect on the origin of this fear or belief. Where did it come from, and how has it influenced your thoughts and actions?*
- *Challenge the validity of this fear or belief. Is there evidence to support it, or is it based on assumptions or past experiences?*
- *Brainstorm potential strategies for confronting and overcoming this fear. How can you gradually expose yourself to the fear in a safe and manageable way? Write down a plan of action for overcoming this fear and achieving your goals.*

3. ***Comfort Zone Expansion:***

- *Identify one area of your life where you feel stuck or stagnant, possibly due to staying within your comfort zone.*
- *Reflect on the benefits of stepping outside of your comfort zone in this area. What opportunities for growth and development lie beyond your current boundaries?*
- *Identify one small, manageable step you can take to expand your comfort zone in this area. It could be trying a new activity, initiating a conversation with someone new, or taking on a new challenge.*
- *Commit to taking this step within a specific timeframe. Write down how you will overcome any fears or doubts that may arise and visualize yourself successfully stepping outside of your comfort zone.*

4. ***Goal Setting and Action Planning:***

- *Identify one transformational goal you would like to achieve in the near future. Make sure it is specific, measurable, achievable, relevant, and time-bound (SMART).*

- *Break down this goal into smaller, actionable steps. What are the specific tasks or actions you need to take to move closer to achieving this goal?*
- *Prioritize these steps and create a timeline for completing them. Set deadlines for each step to keep yourself accountable and motivated.*
- *Reflect on potential barriers or obstacles you may encounter along the way. How can you proactively address these challenges and stay on track towards achieving your goal?*

These interactive exercises and reflection prompts can help you apply the strategies discussed in this chapter and apply it your own lives, deepen your understanding of the material, and take concrete steps towards overcoming obstacles and thriving in the face of adversity.

Allowing Yourself to Forgive

Forgiveness is a deeply transformative act that involves letting go of feelings of resentment, anger, or vengeance towards oneself or others who have caused harm. At its core, forgiveness is about releasing the emotional burden of past grievances and finding peace within oneself. It is a conscious choice to move forward with compassion and empathy, regardless of the pain inflicted. In the journey of personal growth and well-being, forgiveness plays a pivotal role in freeing individuals from the shackles of bitterness and resentment. By releasing negative emotions and embracing forgiveness, individuals can experience profound healing and inner peace. Forgiveness allows individuals to break free from the cycle of pain and suffering, enabling them to focus on positive growth and self-improvement. It's important to distinguish forgiveness from reconciliation. While forgiveness involves letting go of negative emotions, reconciliation involves rebuilding trust and repairing damaged relationships. While reconciliation may not always be possible or advisable, forgiveness is a personal choice that can bring about inner healing and liberation, even in the absence of reconciliation.

From a psychological perspective, the benefits of forgiveness are extensive. Research has shown that forgiveness is associated with reduced stress, anxiety, and depression. By releasing negative emotions and fostering a sense of empathy and understanding, forgiveness promotes emotional resilience and enhances overall psychological well-being. Furthermore, forgiveness has been linked to improved relationships, increased self-esteem, and greater life satisfaction. Overall, forgiveness is a powerful tool for personal growth, healing, and cultivating a more compassionate and harmonious world.

Exploring the process of forgiving others involves understanding the various stages and components involved in the journey towards forgiveness. This includes acknowledging the hurt or harm caused by others, recognizing one's own emotions, and making a conscious decision to release feelings of resentment and anger. It's essential to explore the root causes of the conflict or wrongdoing and to seek empathy and understanding for both oneself and the other party involved. Identifying barriers to forgiveness is crucial in overcoming obstacles that may hinder the forgiveness process. Common barriers include feelings of pride or ego, fear of vulnerability, or a sense of injustice or betrayal. By recognizing these barriers, individuals can work towards overcoming them and fostering a mindset of openness and compassion.

Techniques for cultivating empathy and compassion towards others play a significant role in the forgiveness process. This may involve practicing active listening, putting oneself in the other person's shoes, and seeking to understand their perspective and motivations. Cultivating empathy and compassion allows individuals to develop a deeper understanding of the circumstances surrounding the wrongdoing and to foster a sense of connection and humanity. Strategies for letting go of resentment and anger are essential for moving towards forgiveness. This may involve practicing mindfulness and acceptance, reframing negative thoughts, and engaging in self-care activities that promote emotional healing. By releasing pent-up emotions and embracing forgiveness, individuals can experience profound liberation and inner peace.

Case studies and real-life examples of forgiveness in action provide valuable insights and inspiration for individuals navigating their own forgiveness journey. Hearing stories of forgiveness from others can help individuals realize that forgiveness is possible, even in the most challenging circumstances. By learning from the experiences of others, individuals can gain wisdom and guidance on their path towards healing and reconciliation.

Recognizing the need for self-forgiveness is a crucial step in the journey towards healing and self-acceptance. It involves acknowledging past mistakes, shortcomings, or regrets and accepting oneself with compassion and understanding. Self-forgiveness is essential for breaking free from the cycle of guilt and self-blame and fostering a sense of inner peace and self-worth. Common obstacles to self-forgiveness may include feelings of unworthiness, perfectionism, or holding onto unrealistic expectations of oneself. These obstacles can create barriers to self-forgiveness and perpetuate feelings of guilt and shame. By recognizing and addressing these obstacles, individuals can begin to cultivate a mindset of self-compassion and self-kindness.

Practicing self-compassion and self-kindness involves treating oneself with the same kindness, understanding, and empathy that one would offer to a friend or loved one. This may include practicing mindfulness, affirmations, and self-care activities that nurture one's emotional well-being. By embracing self-compassion, individuals can create a supportive inner dialogue that promotes healing and self-forgiveness. Overcoming guilt and shame is a challenging but necessary aspect of the self-forgiveness process. It requires acknowledging past mistakes or regrets without allowing them to define one's sense of self-worth. This may involve reframing negative thoughts, seeking support from others, and practicing forgiveness rituals or ceremonies that symbolize letting go of the past. Tools and exercises for self-forgiveness can help individuals navigate the forgiveness process and cultivate a greater sense of self-acceptance and inner peace. This may include journaling prompts, forgiveness meditations, or guided visualization exercises that facilitate emotional healing and release. By engaging in these tools and exercises, individuals can embark on a journey of self-discovery and transformation, ultimately finding forgiveness and liberation within themselves.

Forgiving oneself for allowing past trauma to dictate the future can be an arduous but transformative journey towards healing and self-liberation. I found myself trapped in a cycle of self-blame and shame, allowing the wounds of the past to shape my present and dictate my future. The weight of unresolved trauma manifested in destructive behaviors, leading me down a dark path of smoking, drinking, and other harmful habits that I am not proud of. Realizing that this was not the life I was destined to live was a pivotal moment in my journey towards self-forgiveness. I came to understand that my past experiences did not define me, and I was capable of breaking free from the grip of trauma and reclaiming my life. It took immense courage to confront the pain and acknowledge the need for forgiveness, both for myself and for those who had hurt me.

Turning to God and seeking guidance from a therapist were crucial steps in my healing process. Through prayer, meditation, and self-reflection, I found solace in the belief that I was not alone and that divine grace would guide me towards forgiveness and redemption. With the support of a compassionate therapist, I embarked on a journey of self-discovery and inner healing, gradually unraveling the layers of trauma and uncovering the strength within me to forgive myself and others. Forgiveness did not come easily, and it required me to muster every ounce of strength and resilience within me. It was a process of letting go of resentment and embracing compassion and understanding towards myself and those who had caused me pain. With each step towards forgiveness, I felt a weight lifted off my shoulders, and I began to experience a newfound sense of freedom and empowerment.

Today, I am grateful for the journey of forgiveness that has led me to a place of mental safety and emotional freedom. While the scars of the past may still linger, I have found peace in knowing that I am no longer defined by them. Through forgiveness, I have reclaimed my power and embraced the possibility of living a great life filled with joy, purpose, and love.

Navigating the stages of forgiveness is a transformative journey that unfolds in various phases, each marked by its challenges and revelations. From the initial recognition of hurt to the eventual release of resentment, forgiveness requires patience, courage, and self-reflection. By acknowledging and navigating through these stages, individuals can embark on a path towards healing and liberation. Coping with emotions that arise during the forgiveness process is a crucial aspect of the journey. As individuals confront past wounds and grapple with feelings of anger, sadness, and betrayal, it's essential to practice self-care and seek support from trusted loved ones or mental health professionals. By allowing space for these emotions to surface and acknowledging their validity, individuals can move through the forgiveness process with greater resilience and compassion.

Cultivating resilience and inner peace is integral to the forgiveness journey. Through practices such as mindfulness, meditation, and self-compassion, individuals can strengthen their emotional well-being and develop a sense of inner strength and stability. By nurturing resilience, individuals can navigate the ups and downs of the forgiveness process with grace and fortitude, ultimately finding peace amidst the storm. Embracing a mindset of growth and self-acceptance is essential for fostering lasting forgiveness. By viewing forgiveness as a journey of personal growth and transformation, individuals can cultivate a sense of empowerment and agency in their lives. Through self-reflection and self-compassion, individuals can embrace their inherent worth and recognize their capacity for healing and renewal.

Reflections on personal experiences and transformation through forgiveness offer valuable insights and wisdom for individuals navigating their own forgiveness journey. By sharing stories of forgiveness and redemption, individuals can gain inspiration and guidance on their path towards healing and liberation. Through reflection, individuals can honor their journey, celebrate their progress, and embrace the transformative power of forgiveness in their lives.

Integrating forgiveness into daily life is essential for fostering lasting healing and personal growth. By cultivating a mindset of forgiveness and compassion, individuals can navigate daily interactions with greater empathy and understanding. This may involve practicing forgiveness rituals, such as journaling or meditation, to release resentment and promote emotional well-being. Maintaining healthy boundaries while forgiving others is crucial for protecting one's emotional and mental health. While forgiveness involves letting go of negative emotions, it does not mean tolerating harmful behavior or allowing oneself to be mistreated. Setting clear boundaries and communicating assertively can help individuals honor their needs and values while fostering healthy relationships based on mutual respect and understanding.

Creating a self-care plan to support ongoing forgiveness practice is essential for nurturing one's well-being and resilience. This may include engaging in activities that bring joy and relaxation, such as exercise, hobbies, or spending time with loved ones. Prioritizing self-care allows individuals to replenish their energy and maintain emotional balance, even amidst the challenges of forgiveness. Building resilience in the face of future challenges is a natural outcome of the forgiveness process. By embracing forgiveness as a tool for growth and empowerment, individuals can develop inner strength and adaptability to navigate life's ups and downs. Resilience enables individuals to bounce back from setbacks and setbacks, fostering a sense of confidence and optimism in the face of adversity.

Celebrating the freedom and liberation found in forgiveness is a powerful way to honor one's journey and acknowledge the transformative power of forgiveness. By recognizing the courage and strength it takes to forgive oneself and others, individuals can cultivate a sense of gratitude and appreciation for the newfound sense of freedom and inner peace. Celebrating forgiveness allows individuals to embrace the present moment and look forward to a future filled with possibilities and potential. Exploring the ripple effects of forgiveness on relationships and communities reveals its profound impact on fostering healing and reconciliation. As individuals extend forgiveness to others, the ripple effect extends beyond personal relationships to ripple through communities, promoting harmony and understanding. By embracing forgiveness, individuals contribute to the creation of a culture of empathy and compassion, where conflicts are resolved through dialogue and understanding rather than retaliation.

Embracing a mindset of reconciliation and healing is essential for fostering meaningful connections and restoring trust in relationships. Through open communication, empathy, and a willingness to listen, individuals can bridge divides and rebuild broken relationships. By embracing reconciliation, individuals create opportunities for healing and growth, both personally and collectively. Advocating for forgiveness as a catalyst for social change is a powerful way to promote healing and transformation on a larger scale. By raising awareness of the transformative power of forgiveness, individuals can inspire others to embrace forgiveness as a means of addressing social injustices and fostering reconciliation. Through advocacy efforts, individuals can contribute to the creation of a more just and compassionate society. Continuing the journey of personal growth and spiritual evolution is an ongoing process that is deepened through the practice of forgiveness. As individuals commit to their own growth and healing, they create space for transformation and spiritual evolution to unfold. By cultivating a mindset of openness and self-reflection, individuals can continue to expand their capacity for love, compassion, and forgiveness.

Embracing forgiveness as a path to wholeness and peace is a transformative journey that offers profound benefits for individuals and communities alike. Through forgiveness, individuals can heal past wounds, restore relationships, and create a more compassionate and harmonious world. By embracing forgiveness as a guiding principle in their lives, individuals can experience greater fulfillment, resilience, and inner peace, ultimately contributing to the creation of a more peaceful and just world for all.

Sustaining Growth and Fulfillment

In today's fast-paced and often demanding world, prioritizing self-care has become more crucial than ever. Yet, amidst the hustle and bustle of daily life, it's easy to overlook our own well-being in favor of meeting external obligations and responsibilities. This chapter aims to address this imbalance by introducing a practical exercise designed to create a comprehensive self-care plan that nurtures the body, mind, and soul. At its core, self-care is about intentionally nurturing and replenishing ourselves on a physical, mental, and emotional level. It's about recognizing our own needs and taking proactive steps to meet them, ensuring that we can show up fully present and engaged in our lives. However, while the concept of self-care is widely embraced, many struggle to translate it into tangible actions that fit seamlessly into their daily routines.

To bridge this gap, this chapter dives deep into the practical aspects of creating a personalized self-care plan. By providing specific examples of self-care activities for the body, mind, and soul, readers will gain a clear understanding of what self-care looks like in practice. From simple physical exercises to promote movement and vitality to mindfulness practices that cultivate mental clarity and emotional resilience, the goal is to offer a diverse range of options that resonate with readers' individual preferences and needs. Mere knowledge of self-care activities is not enough; implementation is key. Therefore, this chapter goes beyond mere suggestions by offering practical guidance on how to incorporate these activities into daily routines effectively. Whether it's carving out dedicated time for self-care amidst busy schedules or integrating small moments of mindfulness into everyday tasks, readers will learn strategies to make self-care a non-negotiable part of their lives.

Ultimately, the self-care plan outlined in this chapter serves as a roadmap to holistic well-being, empowering readers to prioritize their own needs and cultivate a sustainable foundation for growth and fulfillment. By engaging in regular self-care practices that nourish the body, mind, and soul, readers will not only enhance their overall quality of life but also foster a deeper sense of connection with themselves and the world around them.

1. ***Body:***

Physical Exercise: Engage in regular physical activity such as walking, jogging, yoga, or strength training to boost physical health and energy levels.

Healthy Eating: Prioritize nutritious foods like fruits, vegetables, lean proteins, and whole grains to fuel your body and promote overall well-being.

Adequate Rest: Ensure you get enough sleep each night to allow your body to rest and rejuvenate, aiming for 7-9 hours of quality sleep.

2. ***Mind:***

1. *Mindfulness Meditation: Practice mindfulness meditation to cultivate present moment awareness, reduce stress, and enhance mental clarity.*
2. *Journaling: Dedicate time each day to journaling to reflect on your thoughts, emotions, and experiences, fostering self-awareness and emotional resilience.*
3. *Learning and Growth: Engage in activities that stimulate your mind, such as reading books, learning a new skill or language, or solving puzzles.*

3. ***Soul:***

1. *Gratitude Practice: Take time each day to express gratitude for the blessings in your life, fostering a sense of appreciation and contentment.*
2. *Spiritual Connection: Connect with your spiritual beliefs and practices, whether through prayer, meditation, attending religious services, or spending time in nature.*
3. *Creative Expression: Explore creative outlets such as painting, writing, music, or gardening to nourish your soul and foster self-expression.*

Incorporating these activities into daily routines can be achieved by setting aside dedicated time slots for self-care practices. For example:

1. *Schedule a morning walk or yoga session to kickstart your day with physical activity and mindfulness.*
2. *Set aside time during lunch breaks or evenings for journaling or reading to unwind and reflect on your day.*
3. *Allocate time before bed for relaxation techniques such as meditation or gratitude journaling to promote restful sleep and inner peace.*

It's important to personalize your self-care plan based on your individual preferences, priorities, and schedule. Experiment with different activities and routines to find what works best for you, and don't hesitate to adjust your plan as needed to ensure it remains sustainable and fulfilling. By prioritizing self-care and incorporating these practices into your daily life, you can cultivate holistic well-being and support your ongoing growth and fulfillment.

Sustaining growth and fulfillment requires embracing change as an integral part of life's journey. Adapting to new circumstances, overcoming obstacles, and seizing opportunities demand flexibility. This adaptive mindset empowers individuals to navigate challenges resiliently, transforming setbacks into opportunities for growth. Cultivating an attitude of adaptability enables individuals to sustain momentum and continue progressing toward their goals, even amidst uncertainty.

Additionally, sustaining growth and fulfillment hinges on cultivating self-awareness and engaging in regular reflection. Self-awareness is pivotal in assessing progress, identifying areas for improvement, and aligning actions with values and aspirations. Through introspection, individuals gain insights into their strengths, weaknesses, and motivations, enabling informed decision-making and course corrections along the journey. Cultivating self-awareness empowers individuals to stay authentic and maintain purpose and direction amidst life's vicissitudes.

Prioritizing self-care and well-being is another cornerstone of sustaining growth and fulfillment. Attending to physical, mental, and emotional health is vital for maintaining energy, focus, and resilience. Whether through exercise, mindfulness practices, or nurturing relationships, prioritizing self-care enables individuals to recharge and stay grounded amidst life's demands. By making self-care a priority, individuals sustain their growth trajectory and prevent burnout or stagnation along the way.

Moreover, building supportive networks and communities is instrumental in sustaining growth and fulfillment. Surrounding oneself with like-minded individuals, mentors, and peers provides valuable encouragement, accountability, and perspective. These connections offer a sense of belonging and camaraderie that fuels personal development. By nurturing supportive networks, individuals sustain motivation and momentum on their journey toward fulfillment.

Finally, sustaining growth and fulfillment entails celebrating progress and milestones along the way. Acknowledging achievements, regardless of size, reinforces positive behaviors and motivates continued effort. Celebrating progress fosters gratitude and fulfillment, reminding individuals of their journey's milestones. By pausing, reflecting, and celebrating accomplishments, individuals renew their sense of purpose and commitment to sustaining growth and fulfillment in the long term.

Creating a long-term plan for personal development is essential for individuals seeking to achieve their goals and maximize their potential. A comprehensive plan provides a roadmap for growth, guiding individuals through a series of actionable steps designed to foster continuous improvement and self-fulfillment. First and foremost, crafting a long-term plan begins with introspection and self-assessment. Individuals must reflect on their values, strengths, weaknesses, and aspirations to gain clarity about their desired direction. By identifying areas for growth and setting meaningful goals aligned with their values, individuals lay the foundation for their personal development journey.

Once goals are established, it's crucial to break them down into smaller, manageable tasks and milestones. This approach allows individuals to track their progress effectively and maintain momentum as they work towards their objectives. Breaking down goals also makes them less daunting and more achievable, increasing motivation and confidence along the way. A long-term plan should incorporate strategies for skill development and continuous learning. Whether through formal education, training programs, or self-study, acquiring new knowledge and honing existing skills is key to personal growth. By committing to lifelong learning, individuals stay adaptable and competitive in a rapidly changing world, positioning themselves for success in their chosen endeavors.

Additionally, integrating accountability measures into the plan can enhance its effectiveness. Sharing goals with trusted friends, mentors, or coaches can provide valuable support and encouragement, as well as hold individuals accountable for their progress. Regular check-ins and progress reviews help individuals stay on track and adjust their approach as needed, ensuring they remain aligned with their long-term objectives. Flexibility is essential when creating a long-term plan for personal development. Life is unpredictable, and circumstances may change, requiring individuals to adapt their plans accordingly. By remaining open-minded and willing to adjust course as necessary, individuals can navigate challenges and setbacks with resilience, ultimately staying focused on their journey towards self-improvement and fulfillment.

Reflecting on progress and celebrating achievements is a vital component of personal development, providing individuals with valuable insights into their journey of growth and self-improvement. Taking the time to pause and assess one's progress allows for a deeper understanding of the strides made and the challenges overcome along the way. Reflection provides an opportunity to acknowledge and appreciate the milestones achieved. Whether big or small, every accomplishment deserves recognition. By celebrating achievements, individuals cultivate a sense of pride and motivation, fueling their determination to continue pursuing their goals.

Taking time to look back on progress allows us to evaluate what has gone well and where we might need to make adjustments. It's a chance to learn from both our triumphs and our challenges, gathering valuable insights that can guide our future choices. By honestly assessing ourselves, we can pinpoint our strengths to build on and areas where we can grow, refining our strategies for even better outcomes. Moreover, celebrating our accomplishments brings a sense of joy and resilience. When we focus on what we've achieved, it boosts our confidence and fills us with optimism for what lies ahead. This positive mindset becomes a driving force, inspiring us to keep going even when faced with difficulties.

The process of reflecting on progress allows individuals to assess what has worked well and what areas may require further attention or adjustment. It offers a chance to learn from both successes and setbacks, gaining valuable lessons that can inform future actions and decisions. Through honest self-assessment, individuals can identify strengths to leverage and areas for growth to address, refining their approach for even greater success. Furthermore, celebrating achievements fosters a positive mindset and cultivates resilience in the face of challenges. By focusing on past successes, individuals build confidence in their abilities and develop a sense of optimism about their future prospects. This positive outlook serves as a powerful motivator, empowering individuals to persevere in the face of obstacles and setbacks.

Lastly, reflection and celebration foster a sense of gratitude for the journey itself and the support received along the way. Recognizing the contributions of others, whether mentors, friends, or family members, reinforces the importance of community and connection in personal growth. It reminds individuals that they are not alone on their journey and encourages them to pay it forward by supporting others in their pursuit of personal development.

Finding meaning and purpose in life is a deeply personal journey that often involves introspection and exploration. It begins with a fundamental question: What gives our lives meaning? For some, it may be the pursuit of personal goals or aspirations, while for others, it could involve serving others or contributing to a cause greater than themselves. This quest for meaning drives us to seek experiences and connections that resonate with our core values and beliefs. One approach to finding meaning and purpose is through self-discovery and reflection. By taking the time to understand ourselves—our passions, strengths, and values—we can uncover what truly matters to us. This self-awareness allows us to align our actions and choices with our innermost desires, leading to a greater sense of fulfillment and purpose in life.

Another avenue for finding meaning is through relationships and connections with others. Building meaningful connections with friends, family, and community members can provide a sense of belonging and purpose. Whether through acts of kindness, collaboration on shared goals, or simply offering support and empathy, these connections enrich our lives and give us a sense of purpose beyond ourselves. Engaging in activities that challenge and inspire us can also contribute to our sense of meaning and purpose. Whether it's pursuing a hobby or passion project, volunteering for a cause we believe in, or embarking on a journey of personal growth and self-improvement, these experiences can bring a profound sense of fulfillment and satisfaction.

For many people, spirituality and faith play a central role in finding meaning and purpose in life. Belief in a higher power or connection to a spiritual community can provide a framework for understanding the meaning of existence and one's place in the world. Practices such as prayer, meditation, or religious rituals can offer solace, guidance, and a sense of belonging. Finding meaning and purpose in life is an ongoing process—one that may evolve and change over time. It requires openness to new experiences, a willingness to explore different paths, and a commitment to living authentically according to our values and beliefs. By actively seeking out sources of meaning and purpose, we can cultivate a deeper sense of fulfillment and satisfaction in our lives, enriching not only our own well-being but also the lives of those around us.

Resilience acts as a foundational element for personal development, empowering individuals to rebound from setbacks and maintain progress during tough times. Confronted with challenges, resilience enables individuals to persist, glean lessons from experiences, and emerge stronger. By underscoring resilience's role in navigating life's highs and lows, we recognize the inherent strength within each person, equipping readers with encouragement and tools to tackle adversity effectively. One effective method to nurture resilience is by fostering a growth mindset. This mindset reframes challenges as opportunities for growth rather than insurmountable obstacles. By perceiving setbacks as temporary and not permanent failures, individuals can approach challenges with increased resilience and determination. Encouraging readers to adopt a growth mindset empowers them to view setbacks as chances for self-improvement, bolstering resilience in adversity.

Practicing self-compassion is another vital strategy for cultivating resilience. Self-compassion involves treating oneself with kindness and understanding, especially in times of difficulty. Instead of harsh self-criticism, individuals practicing self-compassion extend themselves the same care they would offer a friend in similar circumstances. Cultivating a compassionate attitude towards oneself strengthens inner resilience, enabling individuals to navigate adversity with greater ease. Seeking support from others is also crucial for building resilience. Establishing connections with friends, family, mentors, or support groups provides invaluable encouragement, guidance, and perspective during tough times. By seeking support when needed, individuals can draw strength from relationships and collective wisdom, navigating life's challenges with resilience and grace. Encouraging readers to cultivate supportive networks and reach out for help fosters resilience, empowering them on their personal development journey.

In addition to emphasizing adaptability and reflection, it's crucial to underscore the importance of resilience in the face of adversity. Resilience serves as a cornerstone for personal growth, enabling individuals to bounce back from setbacks and maintain momentum during difficult times. When confronted with challenges or unexpected obstacles, resilience empowers individuals to persevere, learn from their experiences, and emerge stronger than before. By highlighting the role of resilience in navigating life's ups and downs, we acknowledge the inherent resilience within each individual and provide readers with the encouragement and tools needed to overcome adversity.

One effective way to build resilience is by cultivating a growth mindset. This mindset involves viewing challenges as opportunities for growth and learning, rather than insurmountable barriers. By reframing setbacks as temporary setbacks rather than permanent failures, individuals can adopt a more positive outlook and approach challenges with greater resilience and determination. Encouraging readers to embrace a growth mindset empowers them to see setbacks as opportunities for self-improvement and personal development, fostering resilience in the face of adversity. Practicing self-compassion is another essential technique for building resilience. Self-compassion involves treating oneself with kindness and understanding, particularly during times of difficulty or failure. Instead of harsh self-criticism, individuals practicing self-compassion offer themselves the same care and support they would extend to a friend facing similar challenges. By nurturing a compassionate attitude towards oneself, individuals can bolster their resilience and inner strength, enabling them to navigate adversity with greater ease and resilience.

Seeking support from others is a crucial aspect of building resilience. Connecting with friends, family members, mentors, or support groups provides individuals with a valuable source of encouragement, guidance, and perspective during challenging times. By reaching out for support when needed, individuals can draw strength from their relationships and collective wisdom, helping them weather the storms of life with resilience and grace. Encouraging readers to cultivate supportive networks and seek help when needed fosters resilience and empowers individuals to navigate adversity more effectively on their personal development journey.

Real-life stories of resilience are like windows into the human spirit, revealing our strength and determination in the face of tough times. Let's explore moments where I've shown remarkable resilience, sharing how I tackled challenges and emerged even stronger:

1. *Career Transition:* There was a time, before starting a family, when I was thriving as a phone bank supervisor at Wells Fargo. I loved my job and poured my heart into it. Then came the sudden blow – the call center shut down, leaving me and many others jobless overnight. It was a shock, and I felt the weight of uncertainty and financial worries pressing down on me. But instead of giving in to despair, I saw this as a chance to grow. Drawing on my inner strength, I dove into self-improvement, learning new skills and reaching out to build connections. Despite facing rejections and setbacks, I held onto hope. And eventually, my persistence paid off. I found a new career path that resonated with my passions, bringing a renewed sense of purpose and resilience. This experience taught me that even in the toughest times, there's always a way forward if you keep believing in yourself.

2.***Health Crisis***-During a challenging health crisis, my husband and I were filled with excitement as we embarked on the journey of starting a family. Little did we know, our path to parenthood would be far from easy. When we tried to conceive our daughter Khloe, we were blindsided by the discovery of eight fibroids in my body. Suddenly, I was labeled high-risk and placed on bed rest for the entire pregnancy. Despite my fears, I mentally prepared myself for a cesarean section, knowing it was necessary due to the fibroids obstructing the birthing canal. However, when the medical team at Kings County Hospital disregarded my concerns and attempted to force a vaginal delivery, chaos ensued. With my daughter's heartbeat dropping, an emergency c-section became inevitable. Though they suggested a hysterectomy afterward, I objected, determined to overcome the trauma I had just endured.

Fast forward two years later, when I gave birth to my youngest son, King, the fibroids had multiplied to fourteen. The medical team at Lehigh County Hospital in Pennsylvania warned us of the risks, but with low blood and iron levels, we embarked on the journey with hope. Despite enduring daily pain and discomfort, I remained steadfast in my positivity. After years of living with fibroids, I finally found solace in Dr. Jacqueline Walters, affectionately known as "Dr. Jackie." A beacon of strength and inspiration, Dr. Jackie not only saved my life but also provided the encouragement and support I needed to undergo a hysterectomy safely. She embraced me as if I was her daughter.

In the face of such adversity, I demonstrated resilience by confronting the diagnosis with courage and determination. Despite the daunting challenges, I proactively sought medical treatment, embraced healthy lifestyle changes, and maintained a positive outlook. Throughout the journey of treatment and recovery, my resilience remained unwavering, allowing me to navigate the hurdles with grace and optimism. Dr. Jackie's words, "Listen, I got you. I don't operate in fear, I operate in faith. Good faith. God blessed me to be a doctor and now I in turn will bless you with being able to live a healthy life again," echoed in my mind, providing me with the strength and reassurance to face each day with renewed hope. As a phenomenal black woman who has paved the way in her field as a gynecologist, philanthropist, health expert, and women's advocate, Dr. Jackie's guidance and expertise were invaluable in my journey to recovery.

3. ***Personal Relationships***: When it comes to my relationship with my parents, I've encountered my fair share of interpersonal challenges and relationship turmoil. However, I've consistently demonstrated resilience by prioritizing communication, empathy, and forgiveness. Despite facing setbacks and conflicts, I've remained committed to fostering healthy and meaningful connections. Through open dialogue, self-reflection, and a willingness to compromise, I've navigated through turbulent times, strengthening bonds and deepening mutual understanding.

My resilience in navigating interpersonal challenges has not only enhanced the quality of my relationships with my parents but has also fostered personal growth and emotional resilience. By confronting issues head-on and addressing them with honesty and compassion, I've learned valuable lessons about empathy, patience, and the importance of forgiveness in maintaining healthy relationships. These experiences have shaped me into a more resilient individual, capable of weathering the storms of interpersonal conflict with grace and resilience.

These real-life examples vividly illustrate how resilience has been instrumental in helping me overcome significant challenges and achieve personal growth. By facing adversity with courage, determination, and adaptability, you've emerged stronger, more resilient, and empowered to tackle whatever challenges lie ahead.

Practical Exercise:

1. Create a self-care plan outlining activities and practices that nourish your body, mind, and soul on a regular basis.

Reflection Prompt:

1. How can you cultivate habits and routines that support your ongoing growth and fulfillment?

Embracing Growth: Reflections and Intentions for the Journey Ahead

In the profound journey of self-transformation, characterized by its twists and turns, triumphs and setbacks, reflection and introspection emerge as indispensable companions, guiding us along the path of growth and evolution. As we stand at the threshold of concluding this illuminating expedition into the realms of self-care and personal development, it becomes increasingly paramount to carve out a moment of introspection, to pause amidst the hustle and bustle of life, and to acknowledge the profound strides we've taken and the invaluable lessons we've gleaned. Throughout this voyage, we've delved deep into the intricate tapestry of self-care, weaving threads of mindfulness, resilience, and self-compassion into the fabric of our daily lives. We've explored the myriad dimensions of our being, tending to the needs of our body, nurturing our mind, and nourishing our soul. We've embraced vulnerability as a gateway to authenticity, and we've confronted the shadows lurking within, illuminating the path toward self-discovery and healing.

Now, as we approach the culmination of this transformative odyssey, we find ourselves at a crossroads, poised on the precipice of possibility. It is here, amidst the quietude of reflection, that we have the opportunity to glean insights from our experiences, to distill wisdom from our encounters, and to chart a course forward imbued with intention and purpose. Join me as we embark on the final leg of this journey, a journey not only of self-discovery but of self-actualization—a journey where reflection serves as the compass, guiding us toward the shores of our truest selves. Together, let us pause, let us reflect, and let us embrace the growth that awaits us on the horizon.

    Embarking on your journey of self-transformation is a profound and empowering decision that can lead to lasting personal growth and fulfillment. By applying the principles and practices outlined in this book, you have the opportunity to embark on a transformative path towards becoming the best version of yourself. It's essential to recognize that change begins with a single step, and each small action you take contributes to your overall progress and development. Taking proactive steps toward personal growth and fulfillment requires courage, commitment, and a willingness to embrace change. It's natural to feel hesitant or uncertain about embarking on this journey, but remember that every successful transformation starts with a decision to take that first step forward. By acknowledging your desire for growth and acknowledging your capacity for change, you lay the foundation for meaningful progress and self-discovery.

    One of the most important aspects of embarking on your journey of self-transformation is cultivating a mindset of openness and receptivity to new ideas and experiences. Remain curious and willing to explore different paths and possibilities, knowing that each new encounter or challenge presents an opportunity for growth and learning. Embrace the journey with a sense of curiosity and excitement, knowing that every experience, whether positive or negative, has the potential to enrich your life and deepen your understanding of yourself. As you embark on your journey, it's crucial to set clear intentions and goals that reflect your values, aspirations, and desires. Take the time to reflect on what you hope to achieve and the steps you need to take to get there. Break down your goals into manageable tasks and create a plan of action that will guide you along your path. By setting realistic and achievable goals, you set yourself up for success and empower yourself to make meaningful progress toward your aspirations.

    Throughout your journey, remember to be kind and patient with yourself. Transformation is a process that takes time, effort, and persistence. There will inevitably be obstacles and setbacks along the way, but it's essential to approach these challenges with compassion and resilience. Be gentle with yourself during difficult times, and remember that setbacks are an integral part of the learning process. Use each setback as an opportunity to reflect, learn, and grow stronger.

Finally, embrace the support and guidance of others as you navigate your journey of self-transformation. Seek out mentors, coaches, or like-minded individuals who can offer encouragement, insight, and perspective along the way. Surround yourself with a supportive community of individuals who share your commitment to personal growth and who can provide guidance and encouragement when needed. Remember that you are not alone on this journey, and that together, we can inspire and support each other as we strive to become the best versions of ourselves.

Certainly! Here are some additional resources by Black authors to support your journey of self-transformation:

1. ***Books:***
    1. "The Gifts of Imperfection" by Brené Brown: In this book, Brown explores the power of vulnerability and authenticity, guiding readers to cultivate self-compassion and embrace their imperfections.
    2. "Beloved" by Toni Morrison: This Pulitzer Prize-winning novel delves into themes of trauma, healing, and self-discovery, inviting readers to confront the complexities of identity and history.
    3. "The Four Agreements" by Don Miguel Ruiz: Drawing from ancient Toltec wisdom, Ruiz presents four principles for personal freedom and transformation, offering a path to inner peace and fulfillment.
    4. The Power of Now" by Eckhart Tolle: This book offers insights into mindfulness and living in the present moment, helping readers cultivate inner peace and self-awareness.
    5. "Atomic Habits" by James Clear: Discover practical strategies for building positive habits and breaking free from destructive patterns, empowering you to make lasting changes in your life.

2. ***Online Courses:***

1. "Black Girl in Om" by Lauren Ash: Black Girl in Om offers online courses and workshops centered on holistic wellness, self-care, and self-love, created specifically for Black women.
2. "The Science of Well-Being" by Yale University (Coursera): This course explores the science behind happiness and provides practical tools for increasing well-being and fulfillment in daily life.
3. "Be Well, Sis" by Brittany Josephina: Be Well, Sis provides online courses and resources focusing on mental health, self-care, and personal development for Black women and femmes.
4. "Mindfulness-Based Stress Reduction (MBSR)" by Jon Kabat-Zinn (Sounds True): Learn mindfulness techniques to reduce stress, enhance resilience, and cultivate greater awareness and presence.

3. *Workshops and Retreats:*
   1. "Black Women's Healing Retreats": Explore retreats designed specifically for Black women, focusing on healing, empowerment, and sisterhood, providing a safe space for personal growth and transformation.
   2. "Mindful Self-Compassion (MSC) Workshops": MSC workshops offer training in self-compassion practices to promote emotional resilience, self-care, and overall well-being.
   3. "The Nap Ministry Workshops": The Nap Ministry offers workshops and events centered on rest as resistance, exploring the importance of rest and self-care as acts of liberation and healing for Black individuals and communities.
   4. "Personal Growth Retreats": Explore retreats focused on personal development, mindfulness, and holistic wellness to deepen your self-awareness and transformational journey.

4. *Support Groups:*
   1. "Sista Circle Book Club": Join online or local book clubs like Sista Circle Book Club, dedicated to reading and discussing books by Black authors that promote personal growth, empowerment, and community connection.

2. "Black Therapy Love": Black Therapy Love offers online support groups and resources for Black individuals seeking mental health support, self-care strategies, and community solidarity.
3. Online Forums and Communities: Participate in online forums and communities dedicated to topics such as resilience, self-care, and goal-setting, where you can find support, inspiration, and encouragement from peers.

5. *Tools for Self-Assessment and Goal-Setting:*

- "Black Journaling Prompts" by Alexis Rockley: Use journaling prompts specifically crafted for Black individuals to reflect on identity, resilience, and personal growth, fostering self-awareness and empowerment.
- "Wheel of Life Assessment": Use the Wheel of Life tool to assess different areas of your life, such as career, relationships, health, and personal development, and identify areas for growth and improvement.
- "Black Goal-Setting Planners" by ShineText: Utilize goal-setting planners designed for Black individuals, incorporating affirmations, reflections, and action steps to support your journey of self-transformation.
- Goal-Setting Apps: Utilize goal-setting apps like Todoist, Trello, or Habitica to set, track, and prioritize your personal and professional goals, making progress tangible and achievable.

6. *Personalized Support:*

Therapists and Counselors: Consider working with a therapist or counselor to explore deeper emotional and psychological issues, develop coping strategies, and cultivate greater self-awareness and resilience. Find therapists and counselors from diverse backgrounds who specialize in supporting Black individuals with mental health, trauma, and personal growth.

Mentors and Coaches: : Seek guidance from mentors or coaches who can offer personalized support, accountability, and guidance tailored to your specific goals and challenges. Connect with life coaches and mentors from the Black community who offer personalized guidance, accountability, and empowerment for your journey of self-transformation.

Remember that each individual's journey of self-transformation is unique, and it's essential to explore different resources and approaches to find what resonates best with you. Stay open-minded, curious, and committed to your growth and well-being, and don't hesitate to reach out for support and guidance along the way.

Key Takeaways:

1. Embrace Change: Sustaining growth and fulfillment requires embracing change as a natural part of life's journey. Adapting to new circumstances, overcoming obstacles, and seizing opportunities demand flexibility and resilience.

2. Cultivate Self-awareness: Prioritize self-awareness and regular reflection to assess progress, identify areas for improvement, and align actions with values and aspirations. Self-awareness empowers informed decision-making and course corrections along the journey.

3. Prioritize Self-care: Make self-care a cornerstone of sustaining growth and fulfillment. Attend to physical, mental, and emotional health through practices like exercise, mindfulness, and nurturing relationships to maintain energy, focus, and resilience.

4. Build Supportive Networks: Surround yourself with like-minded individuals, mentors, and peers to provide encouragement, accountability, and perspective. Cultivating supportive networks fuels personal development and sustains motivation on the journey toward fulfillment.

5. Celebrate Progress: Acknowledge achievements, no matter their size, to reinforce positive behaviors and motivate continued effort. Celebrating progress fosters gratitude and fulfillment, renewing purpose and commitment to sustaining growth and fulfillment in the long term.

Throughout the journey of this book, we've explored the transformative power of self-care and personal development, delving into the intricate tapestry of mindfulness, resilience, and self-compassion. Along the way, we've encountered stories of individuals who have bravely embarked on their own paths of self-discovery and growth, overcoming obstacles and embracing change with courage and determination. As we stand on the threshold of concluding this enlightening expedition, it's essential to reflect on some key concepts that have guided us thus far.

One fundamental concept we've explored is the importance of embracing vulnerability as a gateway to authenticity. As Brené Brown aptly puts it, "Vulnerability is not winning or losing; it's having the courage to show up and be seen when we have no control over the outcome." By allowing ourselves to be vulnerable, we open the door to genuine connections, inner strength, and personal growth.

Another crucial insight we've gained is the significance of self-compassion in nurturing resilience and well-being. As Kristin Neff reminds us, "Self-compassion involves treating ourselves with the same kindness, care, and understanding that we would offer to a good friend in times of need." Cultivating self-compassion allows us to navigate life's challenges with greater ease and grace, fostering inner resilience and emotional strength. Furthermore, we've explored the power of intentionality in shaping our lives and creating meaningful change. As Ralph Waldo Emerson famously said, "The only person you are destined to become is the person you decide to be." By setting clear intentions and aligning our actions with our values and aspirations, we empower ourselves to manifest our true potential and live authentically.

In the profound journey of self-transformation, I've encountered my fair share of twists and turns, triumphs and setbacks. One of the most significant challenges I faced was having to confront my own negative attitudes and outlook on life, as well as the anger I harbored towards my parents. It wasn't easy to recognize and acknowledge these aspects of myself, but I knew that true growth required me to confront them head-on. Through introspection and self-reflection, I began to unravel the layers of my emotions, peeling back the surface to reveal the underlying causes of my discontent.

During this process, I turned to quotes and affirmations that resonated deeply with me, serving as beacons of light during moments of darkness. One quote that particularly guided me on my journey was, "The only way out is through." These words reminded me that I couldn't bypass or ignore my challenges; I had to face them directly and work through them in order to emerge stronger on the other side. This mindset shift empowered me to embrace discomfort as a catalyst for growth, rather than shying away from it.

Navigating these challenges wasn't easy, and there were moments when I stumbled and faltered. But with each setback, I learned valuable lessons about resilience, compassion, and forgiveness. I discovered the power of self-compassion in moments of struggle, learning to extend the same kindness and understanding to myself that I would offer to a friend in need. This shift in perspective allowed me to approach my journey with greater gentleness and acceptance, recognizing that growth is a gradual process filled with ups and downs. I'm incredibly grateful for the opportunity to share this journey of self-transformation with you, my readers. Your willingness to embark on this path alongside me fills me with immense gratitude and humility. Together, we're not just navigating the challenges of personal growth; we're forging a community of support, encouragement, and shared experiences. As we continue on this journey, let us remember that we're stronger together, and that every step forward, no matter how small, brings us closer to the fulfillment and authenticity we seek.

In closing, let us draw inspiration from those who have walked this path before us, individuals like Maya Angelou, who famously said, "I can be changed by what happens to me. But I refuse to be reduced by it." Their stories remind us that while transformation may be challenging, it is also deeply rewarding. As we embark on our own journey of self-transformation, may we embrace vulnerability, cultivate self-compassion, and live with intentionality, knowing that every step forward brings us closer to becoming the best version of ourselves.

I hope to have deepened our connection and create a space where we can journey together towards self-transformation with honesty, vulnerability, and compassion. Thank you for being a part of this transformative experience.

Our Last Practical Exercise & Reflection Prompt:

Practical Exercise:

Writing a Letter to Your Future Self:

Take some time to sit down and write a letter to your future self. Reflect on the journey you've undertaken, the challenges you've faced, and the triumphs you've celebrated. Express your hopes, dreams, and intentions for your continued growth and evolution. Be honest and compassionate with yourself as you pen down your thoughts and feelings. This exercise serves as a powerful reminder of how far you've come and offers guidance for the road ahead.

Reflection Prompt:

Lessons Learned and Future Intentions

Consider the lessons you've learned throughout this journey of self-discovery and self-care. How have these experiences shaped you? What insights have you gained about yourself, your needs, and your aspirations? Reflect on how you plan to carry these lessons forward in your life. What changes will you implement? What new habits will you cultivate? Take this opportunity to envision the future you desire and commit to taking the necessary steps to manifest it. The journey of self-transformation is ongoing and ever-evolving. It requires courage, self-awareness, and dedication to prioritize your well-being and personal growth. By engaging in regular self-care practices, embracing change, and cultivating a mindset of continuous learning, you pave the way for a more fulfilling and purposeful life. Remember, you hold the power to shape your own destiny, and with each step forward, you move closer to becoming the best version of yourself.

About The Author

Jaynene Mercer is a multifaceted individual whose life journey has been marked by resilience, compassion, and a commitment to personal growth. As an author, she shares insights drawn from personal experiences and a deep understanding of human nature, offering readers practical wisdom for navigating life's challenges with grace and resilience.

Beyond her work as an author, Jaynene is a successful entrepreneur, owning and operating two black-owned beauty supply stores, a consulting firm, and a non-profit organization dedicated to empowering marginalized communities. Her dedication to social justice and community upliftment is evident in both her professional endeavors and her advocacy work.

A mother, wife, and army veteran, she brings a wealth of life experience to her writing, infusing her work with authenticity, empathy, and a profound sense of humanity. With two degrees—a master's in psychology and a bachelor's in business management—she combines her academic background with her lived experiences to offer readers a unique perspective on personal growth, resilience, and the power of forgiveness.

Through her writing, Mercer invites readers to embark on their own journey of self-discovery and transformation, offering guidance, inspiration, and practical tools for navigating life's complexities with courage, compassion, and grace.

Also by Jaynene Mercer

In the book "The Black Entrepreneur's Guide: The Beauty Business Blueprint", Jaynene Mercer provides invaluable insights and practical strategies for aspiring Black entrepreneurs looking to thrive in the beauty industry. Drawing from her own experiences as a successful entrepreneur and beauty industry expert, Mercer offers a comprehensive road map for navigating the complexities of starting and growing a beauty business.

Through a combination of personal anecdotes, industry insights, and actionable advice, Mercer demystifies the process of building a successful beauty brand from the ground up. From developing a unique brand identity to mastering marketing techniques and navigating the challenges of entrepreneurship, Mercer equips readers with the knowledge and tools they need to succeed in the competitive beauty market.

With a focus on empowering Black entrepreneurs to overcome barriers and achieve their business goals, *The Black Entrepreneur's Guide* serves as an indispensable resource for anyone seeking to make their mark in the beauty industry. Mercer's expertise, passion, and commitment to uplifting aspiring entrepreneurs shine through in every page, making this book a must-read for anyone with a dream of building a thriving beauty business.

Made in the USA
Middletown, DE
21 June 2024

55812685R00060